SHAMANIC
TEACHINGS
OF THE
CONDOR

"This book is of utmost importance. Having studied with Andean teachers for more than fifty years, been initiated by iachaks, and counted Taita Alberto Taxo as a friend, I can confidently say that *Shamanic Teachings of the Condor* is one of the most authentic books on the wisdom, philosophy, and practices of this remarkable man as well as the mystical traditions that date back many centuries. Martha's eloquence, honesty, and humility make this a must-read that's enjoyable for anyone interested in Andean shamanism and provides teachings that are needed today more than ever before."

JOHN PERKINS, AUTHOR OF *SHAPESHIFTING*, *THE WORLD IS AS YOU DREAM IT*, *TOUCHING THE JAGUAR*, AND *PSYCHONAVIGATION*

"This book holds immense value for me both professionally and personally. As a longtime university teacher and researcher, I aim to comprehend global environmental devastation and contribute to its reversal. Martha Travers's insights from the Kichwa people, particularly with Taita Alberto, offer crucial knowledge often overlooked in the U.S. that is essential for addressing our environmental and social crisis. I eagerly anticipate revisiting this book, viewing it as an ongoing resource to deepen my understanding and expand my nature-focused practices both professionally and personally. Martha Travers's instructions and wisdom are invaluable for this endeavor."

JAMES CROWFOOT, PH.D., EMERITUS PROFESSOR OF NATURAL RESOURCES & ENVIRONMENT AND URBAN AND REGIONAL PLANNING, UNIVERSITY OF MICHIGAN

SHAMANIC
TEACHINGS
OF THE
CONDOR

Encounters with
the Mystical Traditions
of the Andes

MARTHA WINONA TRAVERS, Ph.D.

Bear & Company
Rochester, Vermont

Bear & Company
One Park Street
Rochester, Vermont 05767
www.BearandCompanyBooks.com

Bear & Company is a division of Inner Traditions International

Cataloging-in-Publication Data for this title is available from the Library of Congress

ISBN 978-1-59143-506-8 (print)
ISBN 978-1-59143-507-5 (ebook)

Printed and bound in the United States by Lake Book Manufacturing, LLC

10 9 8 7 6 5 4 3 2 1

Text design and layout by Virginia Scott Bowman
This book was typeset in Garamond Premier Pro with HWT Tangent used as the display typeface

To send correspondence to the author of this book, mail a first-class letter to the author c/o Inner Traditions • Bear & Company, One Park Street, Rochester, VT 05767, and we will forward the communication, or contact the author directly at **natureandhealing.org**.

◇◇◇

To
My Beloved Students
May your minds be clear
May your hearts receive beauty
May your future be bright with peace
May your path be the path of service
For all Beings

CONTENTS

Alberto Taxo
Shunguan

CONTENTS

PART TWO

BECOMING A RUNA: PURIFICATION AND SACRED COMMUNION

PART THREE
∧∧∧
THE CONDOR VISITS
THE EAGLE

◇◇◇

FOREWORD

Julia Plevin Oliansky

ONE OF THE GREATEST JOYS IN LIFE is finding our true teachers. These are not necessarily professors or otherwise academic teachers; these are mentors who embody wisdom and can remind us of the truth we know deep inside our hearts but often forget as we walk our daily walk.

I've been lucky in my life to meet a few *real* teachers on my path toward greater harmony with Earth, which I wrote about in my book *The Healing Magic of Forest Bathing,* and so has Professor Martha Travers. When we met (via Zoom, as it was during the pandemic), we recognized in each other a shared language, a shared knowing that is taken for granted in much of the world but obscured here in modern America. Our teachers must have been drinking from the same well, the well of life.

Martha did not just pass by a teacher along her path. She spent over twenty years alongside her teacher, Taita Alberto Taxo, and worked closely with him in both Ecuador and in the United States. *Shamanic Teachings of the Condor* provides a detailed account of Martha's amazing experience of learning from Taita Alberto. He comes to life through the details in her beautifully told stories. Through reading this book, I felt that I, too, had the opportunity to learn alongside him. From detailed accounts of learning the teachings, of carefully prepared meals, of fitful nights of sleep, and of powerful experiences with the volcano Cotopaxi, Martha brings the reader along on her journeys to Ecuador and helps the reader awaken as she does.

Shamanic Teachings of the Condor is a beautiful and desperately needed offering. It represents how the Condor and the Eagle can learn to fly together, harmonizing Indigenous wisdom and Western technology.

As you read this book, you may experience a transformation. There is an energy, a power, in this book that goes beyond the words. You may find that your heart expands, your intuition strengthens, and you begin a process of healing by coming into greater harmony with Nature. *Shamanic Teachings of the Condor* is truly a direct transmission from a great teacher that Martha Travers so eloquently captures on the page for us all to experience. You may find that you begin to see the world anew.

Heed the wisdom in this book—not as theoretical but as living truth—and your life may change. Life on Earth depends on each of us doing our part in the Great Remembering. It starts with remembering the language of the plants and our ability to communicate with the natural world. That's how we become a whole and fully realized human being, "*un ser humano completamente realizado,*" as Taita Alberto would say.

Shamanic Teachings of the Condor is deep medicine for my soul and a book I will be returning to for years to come. Thank you, Martha Travers, for sharing your story and your teacher with us during this precious time.

FOR EARTH,
JULIA PLEVIN OLIANSKY

JULIA PLEVIN OLIANSKY is the author of *The Healing Magic of Forest Bathing,* a creative strategist, guide, and mother. She serves as a devoted mentor and consultant, *a vision doula* to individuals, communities, and organizations, including Fortune 500 CEOs and teams at some of the best brands in the world.

ACKNOWLEDGMENTS

GRATITUDE TO THE MOUNTAINS, Waterfalls, Sunlight, and Wind of the high Andes. Gratitude to Taita Alberto Taxo, Iachak Haskusht Katichik Yuyachik Kausakjuk, for sharing your beauty and wisdom. Gratitude to the families of Kilajalo, Agato, and Membrillo for the loving-kindness you have shared with me and my students. May long life, peace, and prosperity be yours. *Chashna Cachun.*

Many people have supported me on this path. To my first shamanic teacher, Cheryl Stereff, I owe an immense debt of gratitude for teaching me to follow signals and to trust that spiritual forces are always participating in our lives. She and Taita Alberto share the same birth date, the spring equinox.

Gratitude, as well, to Matruka Sherman who called my attention to the Gathering of Shamans where I met Taita Alberto, to John Perkins for bringing Taita Alberto to the University of Michigan, and to Laurie Lytle for hosting the spring 2000 workshop where Taita Alberto invited a small group to come to Ecuador to learn from him.

Deep gratitude to Isabel Contento-Gualan and to Waira, Isabel, and Alberto's daughter for sharing many beautiful journeys with me. Heartfelt thanks to Ecuadorian musicians and iachaks Oscar, Willak, and Rumi Santillan, to their wives, Laura, Mathilde, and Xandra, to their children, and especially to Mama Iachak Maria Santillan, whose deep, earthy peacefulness communicated everything without words. *Yupaichani* to all of you for hosting me and guiding my students over many years of travel.

I wish to acknowledge, as well, the many apprentices and students of Taita Alberto who are walking the path and who have shared their wisdom and knowledge with me and with others. Especially important in disseminating Taita Alberto's work in the United States are Helen, Laz, and Daniel Slomovits, founders of Little Light Publishing, who published several works by Taita Alberto and recorded him chanting and teaching and who also funded a home and intentional community project with Taita Alberto in Ecuador. In addition, the publications of German Rodriguez and Patricia Noriega Rivera in Ecuador have contributed significantly to the scholarly understanding of the mystical traditions of the Andes and to Taita Alberto's role in teaching and healing. Special respect, as well, to Shirley Blancke, whose considerable, tireless effort brought more of Taita Alberto's teachings to the public in her recent book *The Way of Abundance and Joy: The Shamanic Teachings of don Alberto Taxo*. Shirley's book includes many illuminating discussions of Taita Alberto's influence from a variety of perspectives. Heartfelt gratitude to Caty Laignel who hosted Taita Alberto's last workshops in the States, for supporting Taita Alberto and his family, and for sharing her Zoom gatherings with Taita Alberto during COVID.

I would also like to thank Taita Alberto's apprentices: Mama Iachak Vera Lucia Moura for her personal support and guidance as I have walked this path; C. Michael Smith (Mikkal), shaman and spiritual teacher, for his wisdom, friendship, and scholarly contributions to the understanding of Taita Alberto's teachings and the path of the heart; Susan Cooper for her constancy and support of Taita Alberto and his educational mission in the States; and Aileen Kernohan for many years of friendship, sympathy, and understanding.

Special thanks to Itzhak Beery who connected me to my literary agent, Joe Kulin, and to Joe Kulin, himself, whose expertise, guidance and concerted effort brought this book to the attention of Inner Traditions, to Jon Graham for recognizing the value of the book, and to Ehud

Sperling for agreeing to publish the book. Taita Alberto mentioned that he had shared a ceremony with Ehud years ago when John Perkins and Ehud were traveling in the Andes, and it is fitting that Inner Traditions is now instrumental in sharing Taita Alberto's teachings more widely. To each of the caring and professional members of the Inner Traditions staff who have made this book possible, especially to Courtney Jenkins, Erica Robinson, Jeanie Levitan, Emilia Cataldo, and Mercedes Rojas. I owe a debt of gratitude for your marvelous capacity to balance heart and mind—to make available to the world ancient teachings that otherwise might be lost.

Finally, I would like to express my gratitude to Ed Sarath, scholar, composer, jazz musician, and founder of the Program in Creativity and Consciousness Studies for inviting me to teach contemplative studies courses at the University of Michigan. Ed was one of my fellow travelers on my first journey to Ecuador where we met at the home of Taita Alberto. Because of Ed's pioneering work to include the inner dimensions of being in formal academic study, I have had the great privilege of being able to guide students in the nature-based practices of the Andes for almost 20 years.

◈◈◈

> *El mundo necesita este nectar de sabiduria que tu*
> *emanas en el libro.*
> *Tu libro salga a la luz para que ilumine los caminos de*
> *la gente.*
> *Siento que vuelo a esos espacios*
> *del pacha de viajes*
> *y he sentido los aromas de las yervas*
> *Todo es hermoso*
> *Adelante!*

◆ ◆ ◆

The world needs this nectar of wisdom that you
emanate in the book.
Your book emits light so that it may illuminate people's
paths.
I feel that I fly to those places—
of the pacha (time-space) of journeys;
and I have felt the aromas of the herbs
Everything is beautiful
Onward!

TAITA ALBERTO,
EMAIL MESSAGE TO AUTHOR, MAY 22, 2020.

Look at the abundance of nature, of the beauty all around
you, and recognise Me in everything. How many times
during the day as you walk to and fro do you look at
wonders all around you and give thanks for everything?

Much of the time you are in such a hurry you miss a great
deal and fail to absorb these wonders and beauties which
would lift and refresh your very soul.

It is a question of opening your eyes and being sensitive and
aware. Start right now becoming more and more aware of
the things that matter in life, the things that gladden the
heart, refresh the spirit and life consciousness. The more
beauty you absorb, the more beauty you can reflect. The
more love you absorb, the more love you have to give. The
world needs more and more love, beauty, harmony and
understanding, and you are the one to give it forth.

Why not open your heart now and do it?

EILEEN CADDY, FROM *OPENING DOORS WITHIN*

WELCOME TO THE IACHAK FIRE

COTOPAXI, ONE OF ECUADOR'S MOST ACTIVE volcanoes, wears a collar of snow similar to the ruff of white feathers seen on the Condor that nests on its slopes and the white head and neck feathers of the Bald Eagle that lives in the forests of North America. The energies of mountain, forest, and these majestic birds intertwine in the ancient prophecies of the Kichwa people who live along the Andean mountain chain and in areas along the Amazon. In these pre-Columbian prophecies, it is said that five hundred years of peace will prevail when the Condor and the Eagle fly in the same sky.

Near Cotopaxi, in a rural, farming community, visitors from Europe and North America stand waiting for a demonstration of traditional medicine by one of the local healers. This healer, whose traditional title is *iachak,* is preparing to give bee sting therapy to several village residents. It is a cool, cloudy morning. The air is fresh. A light breeze carries the scents of flowering plants and moist earth through the grassy yard of the iachak's home where his family has lived for generations.

The iachak is dressed in a pale lavender shirt and khaki pants. His long, black hair is loose and falls about his face and shoulders. Beside a small thatch-roofed hut are several bee hives painted in various shades of green. Hundreds of bees surround the hives; they seem devoted to their task, entering and leaving the hives with total concentration and ethereal grace.

Two gentlemen and a woman, dressed in traditional clothing—the woman in black skirt, white blouse, and a blue shawl, the men in many-colored ponchos and black fedoras—are sitting on the ground close to the iachak at some distance from the hives. The iachak converses with them in Kichwa, listening to their stories, commenting, and laughing. Though the visitors, some of whom are physicians with training in Western medicine, are eager to see this therapy, the Kichwa are in no hurry. They continue visiting as more people from the community enter the yard. Some bring eucalyptus bark for the kitchen fire; others come, perhaps, to see the visitors from strange lands.

After a time, the iachak rises from where he has been sitting with his community, walks over to the hives, and stands quietly among the bees. The bees surround him, some alighting on his chest, shoulders, and back to investigate his shirt, but since the lavender color does not reveal a flower, they fly on. The iachak reaches into the cloud of hovering and flying bees and captures a single bee by its wings. With his other hand, he captures a second. Holding the bees carefully by the wings, he walks over to the woman who is sitting on the ground. She lifts her bare foot up to the iachak. He presses one of the bees against her foot until it stings her and she cries out. The iachak laughs and stings her foot again with the second bee. Then he drops one of the dead bees to the ground and opens the body of the second with his finger. Putting the bee to his mouth, he carefully licks out the honey from its abdomen.

Again, the iachak walks into the cloud of bees, capturing two more, and approaches his visitors offering to sting any of them who want to experiment. No one accepts the offer, but when one visitor's back is turned, the iachak stings him on the back of his knee. This man had been limping since arriving the day before. At the sharp burn of the sting, the visitor hollers and turns angrily on the iachak, yelling at him in words the iachak does not understand, though the tone and gesture communicate quite effectively. Unperturbed, the iachak smiles.

The members of the local community ignore the commotion. Sitting together, they converse quietly, passing a liter of Pepsi around the circle from which each takes a swallow before handing it to their neighbor. The iachak has disappeared behind the family dwelling, and soon his neighbors walk slowly away, still laughing and telling stories. The visitors climb onto a bus and leave for an afternoon at Cotopaxi National Park.

The yard of the iachak's home is quiet now. A few hens wander there pecking at gravel. In the distance, a rooster crows. The branches of the pepper tree that leans over the small dwelling where the women of the family are preparing food stir in the breeze. Tall grasses in the nearby pasture rustle, and the bright light of noon on the equator pierces the clouds. But even as the sun emerges, soft drops of rain fall, sprinkling the earth. All afternoon, in gentle mingling and succession, the elements give their blessings.

In the late afternoon, before the bus of visitors returns, an elderly woman with a white shawl over her head walks slowly into the yard. She is bent beneath the weight of a pile of eucalyptus bark that she has secured to her back with a second shawl. Below her black skirt, her legs and feet are bare. She loosens the shawl that holds the bundle and drops the eucalyptus onto the ground.

For some time, she wanders back and forth from the periphery of the yard to its center, gathering bits of dried grass and twigs, which she piles together with some of the eucalyptus. When all is prepared, she begins singing—a quiet, rhythmic song in which the Kichwa word *nina* can be discerned—and then she lights the fire with a match. The grass flames, the twigs crackle, and the eucalyptus smolders. She drops a small piece of aromatic wood into the fire, saying quietly, *"Yupaichani."*

When the flames have died back and the eucalyptus is burning steadily, she places a small, black iron pot in the fire. In the pot is water; "*Yaku mama za,*" she sings. Into the water, she drops aromatic herbs; "*Ashpamama za,*" she chants. From beneath her shawl, she pulls a feather. It is a large, black Condor feather. She fans the fire; "*Waira mama za,*" she whispers. Small flames burst upward. Surrounding the fire, an aroma of burning eucalyptus, aromatic wood and herbs floats in the soft air as evening approaches. Overhead, high in the sky at a great distance, two birds are circling. Cotopaxi is hidden in clouds. The sun is setting at the same time that it always sets here on the equator, and in the gradually enfolding darkness, the small fire of the iachak burns sweetly.

INTRODUCTION
BECOMING A IACHAK'S APPRENTICE

FOR TWENTY-TWO YEARS, I apprenticed to the South American, Indigenous Kichwa* healer and spiritual teacher Taita Alberto Taxo of the Cotopaxi region of Ecuador.† In February of 2022, he left this life due to complications from COVID. He would sometimes ask me, "Are you ready to die?" He would then follow this question with, "You must be ready to die this moment or to live for a hundred years." Death, to him, was not an ending; it was a continuation of the development of the soul. He referred to death as "leaving the body" and always emphasized: "We are not our bodies. We are that which gives life to our body."

In these days following his death, I have been bringing this manuscript to completion with his help. I feel him in every moment, sending a soft, quiet light to help me on my path. He read many chapters of this

---

*In North America, people are accustomed to seeing this word spelled Quichua. However, it often is spelled Kichwa in literature published in Ecuador, and the Indigenous people I have studied with prefer Kichwa as they say the letter *k* replacing *qu* and *wa* replacing *ua* more accurately represent the actual sound in the Kichwa language. In Peru the language of the Quichua people is called Quechua and is pronounced accordingly. In Ecuador both the name of the people and the name of their language is Quichua or Kichwa.

†*Taita* is an honorific title that literally means "father." When used as a title, it refers to the person's high level of spiritual development.

1

book and was keen on sharing it with the world. "You write from the heart," he would say. "It is not theory that you speak; it is experience." My hope is that the stories and teachings that I share here will spread Taita Alberto's influence more broadly. Central to his path was his commitment to helping human beings return to intimate communion with this beautiful Earth. I invite you to walk with me and to walk with Taita Alberto into the world of an Andean mystic, to feel what I have felt, to learn what I have learned.

Taita Alberto taught traditions of deep respect for all of life. This includes a profound knowing—born of intuitive feeling—that we live in a world peopled by many beings whose outward appearance is different from our own but who are equal members of creation nonetheless. These beings sometimes appear as mountains; sometimes as clouds, thunder, and rain. They manifest as rocks, plants, birds, insects, animals, fish, and reptiles. Even the objects that the Western world calls inanimate are understood to possess forms of consciousness quite different from human but real nonetheless—for example, minerals such as quartz crystals and silicon and, yes, even human-made objects such as computers. All of the material world is understood to participate in the great cosmic field—a field that is awake. To remind human beings of their proper place in this world of many beings was a central aspect of Taita Alberto's path.

Born in 1954, Taita Alberto was given a Spanish name because at that time it was illegal in Ecuador to give one's child an Indigenous name. Thus, his birth name was entered in the legal records as Luis Alberto Taco Chicaiza—Taco being his father's last name and Chicaiza his mother's. But over time, as the elders recognized special traits in the growing child and young man, he was given four Indigenous names: Haskusht, "one who calls, one who invites"; Katichik, "one who lights the fire, who initiates, who makes it continue"; Yuyachik, "one who helps us remember"; and Kausakjuk, "one who does the practices; one who lives it."[1] His last name Taco was changed to Taxo because the elders saw a similarity with the taxo flower that bears masculine and feminine qualities combined within the same form and that flowers continuously.

Sometimes referred to as a shaman, Taita Alberto was known by his people as a *iachak*.* He was called a *taita*, or father, iachak because he was also a teacher of iachaks and a spiritual and political leader for his community. Taita Alberto's responsibilities extended beyond the role of the iachak, who tends individual ills and imbalances within the community, to caring for the current and future condition of all of the Kichwa people throughout the Andes and, at its most extensive, to caring for the well-being of all the creatures and elements of Earth herself. In his most extensive role, Taita Alberto was responsible for sharing the ancient teachings of his pre-Inca ancestors—the Jatun Taita Iachaks— the Very High Father Iachaks—to all who were ready to learn.

These ancient Jatun Taita Iachaks foresaw the coming of the Spaniards, predicting an invasion that would severely destabilize the Indigenous communities. In preparation for this great change, which the Jatun Taita Iachaks saw as inevitable, Taita Alberto's ancestors put the deep, mystical teachings "to sleep," hiding them from the invaders in order to preserve them for future times. To put a teaching to sleep also meant to no longer share the teaching widely, even within the Indigenous community. In part, this was to protect the Indigenous people who were subject to slaughter if caught practicing their ancient rites. In addition, limiting who was taught the traditions meant saving them for the future, as one might bury a seed deep in the earth, knowing with certainty that a time will come when it will again bear fruit. Notable in Taita Alberto himself and in the mystical teachings is patience born of trust in the timing of the universe—a recognition that

---

*There are variant spellings of this word, including *iachag, yachag, iachak,* and *yachak.* I use the *ia* spelling because this is how Taita Alberto spelled it in the many emails and other communications he shared with me over the years. In English pronunciation, *ia* sounds like the *ya* syllable in yahoo. This is why I will write "a iachak" instead of "an iachak."

everything moves in cycles—a time of building followed by a time of undoing followed by a time of building again. This trust is a constant in the shamanic teachings that I have been exposed to.

So it was that for a period of five hundred years, the Taita Iachaks, through visioning and ceremony, discovered those individuals within each generation who had the skills and the soul necessary to learn the teachings, to guard them, and then to pass them on to the next generation, maintaining certain secrets and codes that to this day are only shared with a few.

Taita Alberto was descended in a direct line through both his father and his mother from the ancient Jatun Taita Iachaks, and though he has said that if given a choice he would not have chosen the path of the iachak, when he was told by his elders that he must enter the ceremony of initiation, he had such great respect for them that he could not say no. The elders perceived that Taita Alberto had the gift of genuine feeling, which includes the ability to merge with other beings through compassion. They recognized, as well, his keen intellect. But, most importantly, they perceived at a soul level that Taita Alberto bore the mark of Atau Alpa, the great Incan hero whose name signifies one whose power is so great that he is able to maintain the equilibrium of Earth herself. In Taita Alberto, the elders recognized the return of this ancient Jatun Taita Iachak. Those of us who walked with Taita Alberto would sometimes hear him chant the Kichwa words of his ancestors that prophesied the return of the ancient ones: *"Waranga Waranga! Kutin Shamushun!"* (By the thousands and thousands again we will come!)[2]

In the 1970s, when in his early twenties, Taita Alberto was initiated as a iachak by his elders. Over time, as his capacities developed, his responsibilities increased. His role in the Indigenous uprising of 1990 is well known in Ecuador. Urged by his people to speak, Taita Alberto presented a list of demands in a public forum, while thousands of people listened and cheered. Even then his gentleness and humor were apparent, as can be seen in a video recording of his speech, given in Ecuador in 1990.[3]

The movements of life and the nature of the times into which he was born added an unexpected responsibility for Taita Alberto. His elders told him that the time would come when he would be traveling to North America and Europe. They told him that he would be teaching non-Indigenous people how to reconnect with Earth. When the elders told him this as they sat around a fire in a remote Andean village, the young Alberto found it difficult to believe. He had traveled to Peru, Bolivia, Colombia, and Mexico to learn from wisdom teachers there, but these journeys were part of his early training and were to visit Indigenous peoples like himself. He could not understand how it would come to pass that he would be traveling to non-Indigenous communities, and he doubted that he would find people in those communities who would wish to learn. But in spite of his doubt, he also knew from experience that when the elders told him something would happen, it did.

So it was that in 1989, the year the Berlin Wall fell, Indigenous elders along the Andean mountain chain, in the Amazon, through Central America, Mexico, and North America passed word that the time had come for ancient prophecies to be fulfilled, and at that time, Taita Alberto's elders told him of the important role he was to play in activating these prophecies.

To the elders of the Kichwa people of Ecuador, fulfillment of these prophecies had long been awaited. The prophecy spoke of a time when people from two vastly different cultures would come together to share and to learn. These cultures, called the Condor and the Eagle, were understood to be carriers of two great capacities that, over time, had become separated from each other and needed to be reunited.

The Condor's gift—the power of the *heart*—and the Eagle's gift—the power of the *mind*—are two halves of a whole. United, heart and mind had ensured the survival of the human species. From earliest times, daily survival for *Homo sapiens* had required the use of both powers. For centuries, the Condor and the Eagle had flown together in the same sky. Living from the heart, the Condor felt intimate connection with all of life. Living from the mind, the Eagle applied intelligence and reason to resolve the practical difficulties of everyday living.

With heart and mind working in unison, the capacities of intellect and reason were guided by the intelligence of the heart. The well-known question of North American Indigenous teachers—Will it be good seven generations hence?—is an example of heart and mind working together. When mind proposed an innovation, a new technological possibility, it would not be automatically assumed that it offered progress. Instead, the elders would seek to know the impact of that innovation in the future—as far into the future as seven generations—and if it was not clear that the innovation would be good for of "all our relations," then the innovation would not advance. Critical to this process of decision-making was the emphasis on certainty. If there was any doubt about the long-term effect, the answer would be "no, we will not do this." This is the role of the heart—to feel its intimacy with the Earth and to prioritize the continuation of Life.

However, over time, these two great powers have diverged to the degree that some now continue to live in intimate connection with the Earth while others live as if the Earth does not matter.

The Kichwa date the severing of the capacities of heart and mind to the era that began with the European invasion of their homeland in the fifteenth century. In the mystical tradition of the Andes, historical time is perceived to move in five-hundred-year epochs called *pachas*. Taita Alberto's pre-Columbian elders foresaw the coming era of dissolution, which they called the *ukupacha*. They knew that during the ukupacha, the world of the Condor would undergo intense stress. But they also knew that the time of darkness would be followed by an era of rebirth, an era called the *nushukpacha*, the era of the dawn. The signs that the elders now recognized pointed to the coming of the era of the dawn. It was this new pacha that was understood to begin in the late 1980s.

When elders of Indigenous communities throughout the Americas recognized the beginning of this new era, they realized that this was the time for the people of the Condor to reach out to the people of the Eagle. Striving to rise ever higher, the Eagle had flown too far from the Earth. Now, the heart of the Condor sought to help the mind of the Eagle return to its ancient bond with the Earth.

To return heart and mind to a shared, equal relation is the medicine that the Kichwa elders prescribed for the new pacha, but how was this to be accomplished? How to help the Eagle learn again to live from the heart? How to *teach* balance between heart and mind? The elders knew that the heart opens through energetic activations that occur when a human being is immersed in the natural world. They also recognized in Taita Alberto an adept who was gifted with the ability to activate the heart through what mystics call the direct transference of spirit.

These two influences—immersion in the natural world and Taita Alberto's ability to directly transmit the heart-connected state of being—were the keys the elders sought to unlock the heavy door of the Western tradition's increasing reliance on mental abstractions, technology, and subjugation of the natural world. Taita Alberto was instructed to begin sharing with those non-Indigenous people who wished to learn. He was told that large groups were not necessary. Small, intimate groups would create powerful medicine that would radiate out beyond the individual people as each of them began to awaken their heart energy.

Small groups of teachers and apprentices were the ancient way, and Taita Alberto was encouraged to maintain this ancient form. In the early 1990s, Taita Alberto traveled to the United States for the first time, teaching in North Carolina. He loved the experience of meeting the Eagle and sharing the beginning teachings. He said he often felt that he was flying. He knew that he was activating the dream of the Jatun Taita Iachaks, and this made him very happy. Nevertheless, he found the effects of travel in airplanes, life in cities, and the level of need expressed by the individuals who attended his workshops very draining of his physical energy. Upon returning to Ecuador after his first journey to the States, he went up into the mountains to a very remote location and stayed there for many weeks to restore his energy. He decided that he did not wish to travel to the States often, and he began to invite people to come to Ecuador to study with him both to retain his own energy and also to encourage the Eagle to experience, firsthand, the life and energetic field of the Condor.

I met Taita Alberto in 1999 when, at the request of John Perkins, author of *The World Is As You Dream It* and founder of Dream Change Coalition, Taita Alberto traveled with a group of medicine people from the Amazon and Andes to speak at a conference on alternative medicine at the University of Michigan Medical School.[4] I attended a weekend of healing ceremonies following this conference, and it was at the opening fire ceremony that I encountered Taita Alberto.

My first journey to Ecuador, which is described in chapter 2, happened in the fall of the year 2000. Subsequently, I traveled often to Ecuador to learn the mystical teachings of the Andes. My early shamanic teachers—Cheryl Stereff, Sun Bear, Brooke Medicine Eagle, and Rolling Thunder—all helped me understand an essential teaching of Earth-based peoples—the principal of reciprocity with the natural world. It was this principal and my desire to help people of industrialized cultures reconnect with Nature that inspired my path and motivated me to learn how to help people stop harming our beautiful Earth home.

A person can want to change, but they may not know how.* The key to leaving our destructive habits behind and what Taita Alberto teaches is activation of the heart: what this means will be shown throughout this book. But here it is important to emphasize that this is not refer-

---

*Throughout this book, the pronouns *they* and *them* are used when an unspecified person is referred to or discussed.

ring to intensifying one's emotions; quite the reverse. Emotions come from the mind, not from the heart. To activate the heart means to activate the energetic bond that we share with all beings. This bond is felt in mystical experiences. The heart is our intuitive capacity to sense and, thereby, to know with certainty that we *are* Nature, a knowing that can be felt when the mind is quiet, as one experiences in sitting meditation.

In Ecuador, sometimes with others, sometimes on my own, I journeyed with Taita Alberto for days, weeks, and months at a time. These journeys happened over a nearly ten-year period, from 2000 to 2009. During these years, Taita Alberto gave me the great gift of being a guest in the homes of the rural Kichwa. He wanted to share his day-to-day life firsthand. This was incredibly generous of him and of his beautiful families and neighbors. I am still in awe when I reflect on what was shared with me. Coming from the United States, I felt I had gone back in time to the North American agricultural era of the nineteenth century. To live with people who still grow their own food; who raise the cow who gives them her milk; who raise the sheep, alpacas, or llamas who give their wool or hair that is spun into thread and then woven into cloth; and who make their own clothing from that handmade cloth was a great privilege for which I am deeply grateful. I greatly admire the rural Kichwa of the Andes. To witness their incredible skill and the unassuming, quiet manner in which they undertake the most daunting of tasks left me feeling humble and awake.

Evidence of their rootedness in the Earth is everywhere apparent. The agricultural knowledge of the Kichwa is widely admired.[5] Those who farm in the rural areas possess intimate knowledge of the soil, plants, and animals upon which their survival depends. This knowledge has been passed from generation to generation, as have the spiritual teachings, and the two—practical, agricultural knowledge and spiritual tradition—are interwoven. At one time, said Taita Alberto, music was played in the fields while people were working as a form of spiritual practice, harmonizing the people's way of touching the Earth. Today, it is still common for people in the rural communities to know which plants offer medicine and how to use the plants for greatest effect. The Kichwa understand the information communicated to them by birds and other creatures relative to incoming weather patterns and the movements of the restless Earth. They express gratitude to the sun and to the rain, and they listen to messages that come on the wind. The mountains are their ancestors.

At the time I first traveled to Ecuador, the village I visited had no running water or electricity. High in the mountains of the Andes, these very capable people were living in much the same way their ancestors had for centuries. If the economy and great cities of the modern world were to collapse, the rural Kichwa possessed the knowledge, the skill, and the natural resources to survive.

By 2009, the villages I visited had some electricity and indoor plumbing, and many residents had cell phones. In greater and greater numbers, the young people who were born in these villages were moving to the cities to find education, entertainment, and technology. The elders were concerned that the young people were losing vital knowledge of how to survive through daily connection with the land. They were equally concerned that the young were losing understanding of the ancient spiritual traditions. One of the reasons the elders were now inviting people from the outside to come learn these ancient traditions was their hope that the young Kichwa would realize that the modern world they were so curious about was learning to value the world of the Kichwa and was coming to them to learn lessons of how to live in harmony with Earth.

In these communities—primarily Kilajalo south of Quito, Agato north of Quito, and Membrillo farther south near Saraguro—I learned a great deal that cannot be taught in words. Even though I rarely participated in the actual work, I was allowed to be quietly present. Through this process, which Taita Alberto called "walking together," I was able to absorb the mystical teachings in my body, my emotions, my mind, and my spirit. Taita Alberto's teachings happen on every level and are felt in the most simple of activities—preparing and eating traditional foods, washing clothing in the river, walking up mountain paths, feeling the Andean winds, visiting with elder relatives, listening to village council debates, and sitting by the fire to learn legends and teachings. These are the way the Condor teaches.

Most of my journeys to Ecuador were guided by Taita Alberto. In addition to Taita, my teachers in the Andes included elder women, grandmothers of the village who spoke little but watched everything with great intent; young mothers who cared for their children while working all day to keep the family fed and clothed—sometimes carrying large barrels of water from wells hundreds of feet from their homes; and teens who worked in the fields, attended school, and were our guides on long hikes up the mountains to sacred groves and waterfalls.

However, there was a more subtle level of education at work during my travels that transcends any individual human being. At this level, my greatest teachers were the mountains themselves, rising thousands of feet and disappearing into the clouds; boulder-strewn rivers and rushing waters; tiny orchids hiding under fallen bamboo leaves; the brilliant sun rising above the mountains in the morning; the crackling fires we sat around at night; and the colorful birds that sometimes flew into our midst. These elements of Earth, Air, Water, and Fire are the great forces that the elders teach their apprentices to know. And it was from these elements that the greatest teachings came.

As time passed, I began coordinating and guiding groups, bringing them to Ecuador to learn both from Taita Alberto and from other iachaks who had been trained by him. On more than one occasion, these groups were students from the University of Michigan, where I teach contemplative studies, who traveled with me to Ecuador to share in the rural life and to learn some of the teachings. The more deeply I worked with Taita Alberto, the more frequently I traveled alone with him, high up into the mountains to visit people he loved and to sit for days at a time in the majestic Andean highlands in meditation and solitude. Over the years, what I learned has become part of my being—a transformation at a cellular level.

Taita Alberto also taught frequently at my home in the Michigan woods. Beginning in the fall of 2000, Taita Alberto offered many beautiful workshops to people who lived in the area or who traveled to Michigan to learn from him. He also visited my classes at the University of Michigan. The summer of 2018 was the last visit he made to me in North America, when he taught a workshop and gave healing ceremonies at my home.

Over the years, Taita Alberto came to my home in Michigan often, sometimes staying for a month or two, during which time he took courses in English, taught workshops, and, for fun, took driver's training, earning a Michigan driver's license. He loved to experiment and would spend hours in area stores examining tools and technological devices. Often he would say, "Any game you want to play."

In 2004, Taita Alberto asked me to begin a school with him and suggested that it be called the Winona Taxo University. He took me to a house that he had designed and built in the rural Kichwa community, Membrillo, which he called La Casa del Saber Ser, or the House of Knowing How to Be, and he shared with me his dream of using this house as a center where the Eagle and the Condor could meet to exchange their gifts.

We moved forward and created a website for the university. Taita Alberto was closely involved in important details, such as the colors that were used on the site. At approximately this time, we also began an online school together. Students were given practices to do each month, and at the end of the month, they wrote to Taita Alberto about what they had experienced, and he wrote back. The university and the online school faltered after a few years because Taita Alberto had moved on to other activities. This was one of the features of working with Taita Alberto that other people experienced as well. Perhaps he thought the

Eagle would take up these projects and carry them forward, but when he withdrew his energy, the projects did not always continue or they shape-shifted into another form, with other students carrying them forward. I always trusted that what needed to grow would grow.

Taita Alberto was adept at initiating projects, and he was also peaceful about letting them go if they did not energize. He would often say, "We are learning together by experimenting. It is good to try things. But we do not have to force. We do not have to walk with a lot of weight on our shoulders. If it does not feel light, if it does not fly, then you can let it go." And then he would touch my face and playfully add, "*No es necesario preocupar la mente de Mar dha.*" (It is not necessary to worry the mind of Mar dha,") a name he had given me that, to him, meant "gift from the sea."

In 2007, spontaneously (I had not requested or intended this) Taita Alberto gave me the title Mama Iachak. Even though I considered myself to be his apprentice, I did not aspire to be called a iachak. To me, that role was the role of an Indigenous Kichwa, not a Caucasian woman who knew herself to be an outsider. I thought of apprenticeship as a continuous process of learning, of walking beside Taita Alberto, but without a goal or agenda. I simply loved being with him. I was absorbing so much beauty as I walked with Taita Alberto. That feeling was incredibly rewarding and washed away any sense of trying to get somewhere or achieve. I was simply in a beautiful state much of the time. Not always, of course, for there were also troubling undercurrents given that we are human beings; but, primarily, I was receiving a great deal.

At the same time, Taita Alberto told me that he would give the title of iachak to those Eagles whom he recognized as capable of sharing his teachings more broadly. When he told me that he wanted to give more Eagles the iachak responsibility, he reminded me that he would only be "in this body" for a brief period of time. He said he wanted to give certain students who had worked with him diplomas—actual, physical certificates that would name them iachaks and would officially confer this responsibility. With the assistance of Susan Cooper, a lawyer whom I had met on my first journey to Ecuador and who had studied closely with Taita Alberto, we created paper documentation of Taita's decision that certain individuals were now ready to take up the iachak duties.

Offering the fruit of my walking with Taita Alberto is one of the ways I reciprocate for what I have been given. As an Eagle, still learning to balance heart and mind, I carry forward teachings of the Condor that make possible the opening of the heart through reintegration with the natural world. When we genuinely feel again that we, *Homo sapiens*, are not an accident but an integral part of Mother Earth, long-held fears begin to dissipate. In addition, the barriers that separate people from their inner knowing begin to dissolve. It is this lessening of fear and awakening of inner wisdom that creates the spontaneous feeling of great happiness, which is the sign that the heart has opened. The person feels joy, spontaneous joy, not because they arrived somewhere or acquired something but simply because they lay down on the Earth and began to feel. This feeling-state is deep and powerful. Every cell of the person's being vibrates in rhythm with the Earth. They no longer say, "We are part of Nature" as an abstraction. They now *know* that they *are* Nature. They have felt their *whole* body, and it includes all beings and forces. This is the mystical experience that erases any doubt.

Part I of this book describes my first journey to Ecuador and the feeling-state that arose in me through experiencing the vibration of the Andean world, a feeling-state that culminated in a sensation of deep serenity in which Time itself disappeared. This first part of the book invites the reader to feel the heart of the Andes—to let go of the Eagle tendency to want to know what, when, and where and instead to journey in the way of dream, storytelling, and poetry. This is how the heart opens. These stories show Taita Alberto, his Kichwa community, and the Andean natural world inviting seekers to attune their attention to a larger dimension of being, to again open the heart, to bring the mind into balance with the heart, and, in doing so, to regain the ability for these two powers to fly in the same sky.

Part II describes in detail specific practices that Taita Alberto taught to his apprentices. These practices purify body and mind and renew our intimacy with Nature. Often, Taita Alberto would say, "The mind will say, 'I need many years in which to learn this.' But these practices come from the heart, and the heart knows how to connect very quickly."

Part III shares the direct teachings Taita Alberto gave at my home and in my university classes. In simple but profound language, Taita Alberto discusses the cosmology of the Andean mystical tradition, his perceptions about the time we are currently experiencing on Earth, and specific practices that open the heart. Taita Alberto's ability to articulate the mystical realizations of his path in words that are poetic and accessible made him an inspiring teacher. His presence and wisdom often communicated so much, even without words, that people left the workshops or classes feeling uplifted and joyful.

Throughout this book, the reader is offered *encuentros*— encounters—a word Taita Alberto used to refer to his workshops when he was teaching in Michigan. The word emphasizes the value and intimacy of the encounter between various persons, between cultures, and between different ways of knowing. These encounters, as I experienced them, were passageways that a iachak travels to visit other worlds or levels of perception, bridges that joined the world of the Condor—the intimate, participatory vibration of the *heart*—with the world of the Eagle—the keen, intellectual perception of the *mind*.

While hosting visitors in Ecuador or while he was visiting us in North America, Taita Alberto offered the gift of traveling with him in the no-longer-ordinary reality of an ancient culture so that we could again experience a way of living and perceiving that all of our ancestors must have known. He invited us to walk with him, not for his own advancement, but to offer to those who were ready an opportunity to experience and return to a way of knowing and being that is ancient

and inherently human. Taita Alberto often said that we are still learning how to become *sers humanos*—suggesting that the condition of
human being is an elevated state that either we have not yet attained or
have lost and must recover.

Ultimately, the iachak in this book is not a human being. The
iachak, the teacher of this healing, is not the Condor or the Eagle.
The iachak is Nature. Nature is who we are. Nature bodies forth our
essence. When we experience ourselves *as* Nature, we experience healing. Mountains teach this. Wind teaches this. Sunlight teaches this.
Waterfalls, lakes, rivers, streams, and the necessary rain teach this. In
the mystical traditions of the Andes as I encountered them, Nature is
the presence through which this connection occurs. For the one who
has lost their way, Nature is the guide. Wherever one lives on Earth,
whether in city or countryside, this great teacher—Nature—is calling
each of us to renew our bond with the Earth, and the ancient, mystical
teachings of the Andes are practical guides to that renewal.

PART ONE

THE EAGLE
VISITS THE
CONDOR

ONE

IACHAK MEDICINE

◆

The Bird People

BEFORE WE WALK TOGETHER in the high Andes, I will share some insights that I gained over the years about what iachaks are, what their responsibilities are, and how they walk their path—or better yet, how they fly.

Iachaks are sometimes called bird people, reflecting their identification with the giant Condors whose power they emulate. Like these immense birds who are rarely seen, the iachak has the ability to "fly"—to move rapidly from one world or condition of consciousness to another.

At the level of ordinary reality, this may mean being able to travel on foot for days, walking from countryside to the city. It may mean retaining one's first language while being forced to learn and speak the language of the colonial culture as well. Developing the capacity to rapidly bridge an immense cultural divide could mean the difference between surviving or not and would include the ability to shift from one worldview to another. Even within the iachak's own community, there may be many, and in some communities it is a majority, who no longer speak the traditional language. Many Kichwa have adopted the colonial religion and at least some of the colonial values and priorities. But not so for the iachak. In spite of the "modernization" of the community, the iachak is challenged to know, to understand, to maintain, and, when called upon, to transmit the ancient traditions of the ancestors.

Significantly, to fly is to develop the ability to travel to other worlds *without being trapped in those worlds.* The Jungian analyst Marie-Louise von Franz expresses this insight:

> The shamans say that being a medicine man begins by falling into the power of the demons; the one who pulls out of the dark place becomes the medicine man, and the one who stays in it is the sick person.[1]

The perspective that is developed in the iachak over time could be likened to the perspective of one standing at the summit of Cotopaxi. From that point of view, multiple locations are visible—multiple worlds—and the iachak is not attached or limited to any single one of them. All are apparent; none are singled out as the "correct" or the "only" point of view. To fly is to have a broad perspective, one that encompasses the many.

At the level of nonordinary reality, the iachak becomes adept at learning the languages of beings other than humans with whom the people share their world. To understand the teachings of bird, plant, waterfall, sunlight, and rainbow is to be able to fly between worlds.

The ability to converse with the many levels of reality includes, as well, the ability to see into other dimensions: to recognize when a person is ill before that person has developed visible symptoms; to know beforehand when an important visitor is coming though the information has not been telegraphed to the iachak via any material world form of messaging; to perceive the best way to keep the community safe in times of revolution and political upheaval; to know before it happens that a volcano will erupt or a storm will wash out the roads or an enemy is coming who means one harm.

The iachak is trained to understand the messages carried in nighttime dreaming or in daytime visioning. These, and many other capacities, are the iachak's way of flying from one world to another.

The world of Nature is the great teacher for the iachak. Nature reveals many levels of consciousness. The many worlds are manifest in mountains, rivers, and waterfalls. They are manifest in maize growing under the sun and in the sunlight itself. They are manifest in the wind and rain that speak and nurture. They are manifest, as well, in city and in country, in buses and gasoline, in cement blocks and thatched roofs, in cell phones and computers. They are manifest in daytime and in nighttime, in sleeping and in waking. The stars and the moon invite participation in different ways of seeing and knowing, just as the sun radiates its own beam of conscious force. Each human culture on the planet carries its unique signature of consciousness, as does each animal, bird, insect, plant, mineral, element, bacteria, virus, and subatomic phenomena.

For the iachak, all beings are understood to be conscious. All beings are expressions of Life, and all beings express themselves. Everything speaks. Everything teaches.

The iachak way of perceiving all things as conscious is one of the characteristics that distinguish the Condor from the Eagle. For those trained in the Western tradition, this perspective can be difficult to comprehend. In the Western tradition, human beings are understood to be at the top of a hierarchy and to possess the highest level of consciousness. While animals, birds, fish, and insects may be granted a certain level of consciousness by the Western scientific tradition, plants are not thought of as conscious, and certainly rocks, waterfalls, and mountains are not.

From the iachak point of view, all material reality is composed of the basic four elements: Earth, Air, Water, and Fire. These elements are perceived to be conscious and, because all things come from these elements, all things are understood to possess "original consciousness." To learn to fly, the iachak must learn the language of the elements, which is why the iachak *listens* to the wind, to the sun, to the rain, to the plants, to the mountains—to all beings.

Listening is an open condition devoid of human projection. The iachak does not imagine or define what the element may be expressing. The iachak learns to separate from human fear and desire—those aspects of ego that create projection—and, instead, enters into a condition of receptivity to the many voices, the many languages of the many beings who share our world.

As a direct result of this practice, the iachak experiences a heightened level of encounter with the world. At this heightened level of encounter, the iachak becomes adept at crossing from one world to another. However, it is not the sometimes perilous yet beautiful flight of crossing from one world to another that is most important. *What is most important is becoming adept at returning to the world of the people and bringing back medicine for those who do not travel.*

In addition to the elements of Earth, Air, Water, and Fire, in the mystical traditions of the Andes, a fifth element is recognized. This element, which could be called a spiritual or etheric element in English, is called *Ushai* in Kichwa. The Ushai is the animating force of the universe; it is the energy that moves Earth, Air, Water, and Fire. Though their ceremonies always invoke Ushai, according to Taita Alberto, the iachaks do not speak of this element often. Frequently, however, they simply use the word *Life* to refer to the energy that animates all things. Again, the cultures of the Eagle, as represented in the Western scientific tradition, do not conceive of everything as having life. But, to the iachak, Life is spiritual energy, and everything possesses both spiritual energy and spiritual purpose.

Unlike traditions of the Amazon where psychoactive plants assist these travels, the iachaks I learned from did not suggest the use of psychoactive plants. They emphasized that journeying arises from intimate communion with the elements of Nature with whom one learns to converse.

Iachaks are trained by Mama (mother) Iachaks or Taita (father) Iachaks. This training may take years before the apprentice is acknowledged as ready to take on the responsibilities of the iachak. It is said that a iachak loses their private self and becomes a public self, that a iachak no longer can take care *only* of their own family but must now care for the whole community. At any time in the day or night, the iachak may be called on to help a person or family in their own community or to travel to other communities to assist people there. The iachak's responsibility includes the entire Indigenous population of the Andes, as the challenges faced by any individual person or community are the concern of every iachak.

Since ancient times, the iachak has been charged with the responsibility of preserving and transmitting the spiritual traditions of the culture. This responsibility includes knowing the special properties of individual plants and foods, knowing ancient legends, and knowing important ceremonies. Most importantly, the responsibility goes beyond knowing in the sense of information that one might hold in one's mind. The responsibility is, ultimately, a responsibility to *feel*, a concept that is difficult to translate into English. What the iachak feels is a deep connection with all of life, a feeling that is said to originate in the heart. This ability to feel means that the iachak can *intuitively* sense the energies that are needed for healing of individuals and communities. This intuitive ability, the capacity of the heart, the energy of the Condor, exists because the iachak is one with the natural world of which they are a part. The iachak is not above Nature and does not control or manipulate Nature. The iachak *is* Nature. It is not the iachak who "heals." It is the energy of Life flowing through Nature that heals.

It is especially important to understand the motivation of the iachak's flight. It is not about self-aggrandizement. The iachak's power is not that of domination or, even, of control. Certainly, the iachak is not flying in order to secure power for themself.* The iachak flies for the community, having relinquished their private, personal gain to serve the larger good. To be a true iachak, one must use one's flying with the express intention of bringing back medicine for one's own community. One might compare this principle to the Navajo recognition that individuals who gain the power to fly but misuse it for their own gain are not healers, but sorcerers.

In the traditional communities, Kichwa women are often the iachaks because they are deeply connected to the heart and to the power of intuition. Woman as iachak reflects the organic processes of nature. Mothers give birth and tend the young, thereby ensuring the continuation of the species. The activities of feeding and healing individuals and of tending community welfare have been the roles of Kichwa mothers and grandmothers for centuries, so it is natural that women become iachaks. Through daily, intimate contact with the origins of life and survival, traditional Kichwa women learn wisdom that, for some of them, finds its natural culmination in the responsibilities of the iachak.

Women create the center of the family, through giving birth, through growing and preparing food, and through the warmth of heart they give. The tradition of many generations living together in one household or in close proximity to one another remains a constant in the rural Kichwa communities, so children are also often cared for by older siblings, by aunts, and by grandmothers as well as by their own mother. This care may include instructing them in reading and arithmetic as well as family lore and local legend, and of course, it includes participating in the family work.

In the rural communities that I have visited in Ecuador, the women work very hard. They plant and harvest the *chacra*—the small kitchen

---

*Throughout the book, the nongendered, reflexive pronoun *themself* is used, instead of *themselves,* when referring to an unspecified individual.

garden outside the house. They care for the animals—typically a cow, sometimes an alpaca or llama. They prepare all the family food, some of it grown in their chacra and the rest obtained at the local outdoor markets that even very small towns have at least two days a week. In addition, the women often carry water in large barrels significant distances from a central village well to the family home. The water is used for all cooking, for household cleaning, and for family baths. Laundry is usually washed in nearby rivers, where groups of women gather to visit and work, standing in the cold water or sitting on large rocks in the rushing stream, conversing with one another while soaping, pounding, and rinsing the family's clothes and while their small children play close by.

The women work with the men in the fields as well, cultivating quinoa, maize, peas, and beans. They participate in the big harvests at the time of Inti Raimi (the celebration of summer solstice). They sell the family's surplus produce in the markets.

Often, the women also make the family clothing—beginning with securing the wool of their own sheep or winding the hair of their own llama onto the distaff and then attaching it to the spindle where it is spun into thread.

In the city of Saraguro in southern Ecuador, women come to market carrying *pushkana*—spindles on which they twist sheep's wool or llama hair into yarn while shopping. Women carrying spindles is an ancient image that has impressed itself upon the human psyche for thousands of years. The spindle is associated with the deepest processes of physical and spiritual life. For example, for the Kogi in the mountains of Colombia, the spindle represents the world tree that sends its roots into the netherworld, its trunk into the world of human endeavor, and its branches into the celestial realm.[2] Just as women hold the spindle, so too, day after day, year after year, women hold the community, its roots, its current life, and its future in their hands.

Through the act of spinning, women wind the many strands of the community together. Traditional Kichwa women, engaged in the process of clothing their families, are not symbols; they are actualities. They *are* the life and continuity of the community.

Each step in the process of making clothing has been experienced close at hand. The wool of the sheep or the hair of the llama may come from a woman's own small herd or that of her neighbors. The women not only feed the animals but assist female llamas when they give birth.

The men also participate in the fabrication of clothing as weavers of cloth. In the community near Otavalo where I stayed at times, it was often the men who operated the wooden hand looms. Indeed, it could be said that the iachak clothes the community in spiritual protection.

While it is often the women iachaks who cure the family's ills with plants gathered from the fields and hillsides and who perform healing ceremonies called *limpiezas*, a traveler from afar who comes looking for a shaman is often introduced to the male iachaks.* While within the communities, the woman's role as iachak is visible, to the outsider, the woman iachak may be so much in the background that she could be said to be invisible.

After traveling to these communities for ten years, my impression is that this was not due to lack of respect for the Mama Iachaks. Rather, it seemed that men having the public face of iachak to those outside the community was an act of protection of the deeper, hidden power of the women.

This appeared to me to be similar to the way Nature protects many bird species. The male has the colorful plumage. He is noticed by potential predators and calls attention away from the mother on the nest whose plumage is the color of the nest and the surrounding plants. Given how many people now come to South America looking for a "big experience" with a shaman, it is understandable that the subtler levels

---

*A *limpieza* is a cleansing. When Taita Alberto did these cleansing ceremonies, he said he was bringing the four elements into balance in the person's being, which then enabled the Ushai to grow.

of spiritual healing are protected and that outsiders are vetted carefully before being introduced to the deeper mysteries.

The iachak possesses a deep knowledge of and respect for the rhythms and processes of the natural world. Both the men and the women in these traditional communities are in daily contact with the elements, the sources of their lives. Experience of the fundamental activities of survival, such as planting and harvesting crops, gathering eucalyptus bark for cooking fires, preparing food, making clothing, building shelters, tending animals, and giving birth creates in the iachak a deep identification with the natural world. Nature is not conceived of as being "out there." Nature is *experienced* as subject—I, myself—not object.

This knowledge translates into the iachak's ability to *go with* the flow of Nature rather than trying to force nature to conform to human convenience. Thus, the iachak has both incredible patience and the ability to act spontaneously to seize an opportunity that Nature has provided in the moment that the offering is made.

According to Taita Haskusht, since the Spanish invasion of the Andes in the fifteenth century, the traditional elders have been safeguarding the teachings that cultivate iachak wisdom. This means that not only did they hide their practices from the conquistadors, they also limited the degree to which they taught the practices in their own communities. Because greeting the sun could mean death if one was seen doing it by the Spanish, the iachaks were careful to train only those in their communities whom they recognized as having the iachak qualities—those who could both guard and pass on the teachings in the right way and to the right people.[3]

Today, Mama and Taita Iachaks only teach some of the most basic practices to outsiders, and they do not teach even these practices to everyone who asks. The person who desires to learn must demonstrate a degree of self-knowledge, humility, and, above all, sensitivity to Nature before the Mama or Taita Iachak will take them on as an apprentice.

It is through first learning to walk that the iachak later learns to fly. Through quiet, patient encounter with the elements of Nature—walking long distances from village to city, from level plain to mountain, and from self-concern to community engagement—the novice iachak gradually strengthens their intuitive understanding of how Life works. It is this intuitive wisdom that gives the iachak wings.

TWO

AT THE FOOT OF COTOPAXI

ON THE AUTUMNAL EQUINOX of the year 2000, I flew to the Andes Mountains of Ecuador with a group of fellow travelers. It was almost midnight when we arrived in Quito. Looking out the window as the plane began its descent, I was startled by the vision of the Earth that I saw below me. When leaving Detroit, I had looked down upon the familiar landscape of carefully-arranged squares. The higher the plane flew, the smaller and more numerous became the squares—row after row of white- or black-roofed buildings lining arrow-straight streets. Soon, we had passed over Chicago and were flying high above the midwestern plains. Here again the pattern of the square dominated. Acres of farmland, carefully parceled out in representations of ownership, order, and planning, lay bordered by slate-colored highways, their firm linearity interrupted only by the Mississippi and its tributaries meandering through the North American continent as if to suggest a possible alternative to our passion for division and carefully-marked boundaries.

But as I looked out my window at the city of Quito below, I did not see a city defined by quadrants. Since it was dark, I could not see the mountains that we were skirting, but as the plane descended, I saw winding trails of soft green and warm yellow lights and knew that they defined the invisible contours of mountain and hill. These were not the bright, white lights that pierce the darkness in North America. Like diffuse, glowing stars, the haloed streetlights followed circuitous paths, traveling up hillsides only to be abruptly cut short, extinguished by the complete dark of the surrounding countryside.

As the plane banked sharply in its narrow course between mountain peaks, the rivers of lights running through the black land seemed to rise parallel to the plane. Here the dominant pattern was not the square but the snake! With the lights in the cabin turned off for landing, we who were new to Quito sat in darkness, while outside our window, snake medicine greeted our eyes.

Intrigued, I gazed at the beckoning lights below hinting that, like the snake who repeatedly sheds her skin, transformation is possible for those who journey in these mountains.

◇◇◇

It was near dawn when we arrived at the home of Taita Alberto. Out of respect for his Indigenous language and ancient history, I use his Kichwa name, Haskusht, in this portion of the book.

Taita Haskusht lived with his family at his ancestral home—the land of his father and grandfather who were also iachaks—in a rural Kichwa community near the great volcano, Cotopaxi. To Haskusht, Cotopaxi was one of his elders, an ancestral guide. His connection with the mountain, the land, the people, the plants, the animals, and the birds was profound. He deeply loved this home, and it was an example of his incredible generosity and that of his family—especially the women who did so much of the work—that they were willing to share this precious place with strangers.

Visitors paid Haskusht and his family with contemporary currency, which made it possible for them to have conveniences like a generator, to hire the bus that picked us up in Quito, and to spend days and weeks guiding us, and, hopefully, to have money left over to repair roofs, pay medical bills, and purchase other necessities. Haskusht would refer to the amenities such as the generator at his home as necessary, not for himself or for his family, but for the visitors from other countries who he feared would not be comfortable without some electric lighting or warm water.

Roosters were crowing as the other fifteen travelers and I headed to our beds. The beds were narrow and close to the floor, the mattresses and pillows stuffed with wool. I barely slept, but drifted in dream.

A few hours later, I rose, not refreshed exactly, but awake. The water in the shower was cold. Haskusht had installed a small, tankless water heater on the exterior wall of the family dwelling. This and the electric lights were powered by the generator. But the machinery was temperamental. The lights flickered often, and during the time I was there, the water heater never worked.

Some days, I saw women carrying water into the kitchen in large barrels slung on their backs with a strap. I never saw the well, so did not know how far they carried this water, but I realized that our visit must mean that they were carrying much more water to the house than was usually necessary.

For breakfast we ate fresh rolls; unsalted, white cheese made from the milk of the cows in the nearby pasture; and a thin, sweet soup made from corn flour and blackberries. In the morning of the first day of our visit, after breakfast, Taita Haskusht called us to join him outdoors under a pepper tree that grew in an area where the grass had been scuffed and torn by the feet of family and community members who used the shade under the tree as a gathering spot. Small tree stumps were arranged in a circle along with two stones large enough to sit on. Haskusht sat on one of the stones. Beside him on the ground was a small handmade drum.

This morning, Haskusht was dressed in traditional clothing— white pants, a white cotton tunic, and a tan, wool poncho with dark-brown stripes running lengthwise. His long black hair was fastened in back. First, he spoke in Kichwa, murmuring quietly in a language that none of us understood, though we could feel the quiet beauty of the sound. Then he began to speak in Spanish. Sara, who had organized our journey, translated for him.

"I do not have a plan," he said and smiled. "Perhaps you thought there would be a plan?" he laughed, then added, "It is good for us to be together. It is good for us to feel the air together, to share food—the gifts of the mother—to enjoy sunlight and moonlight, to sit together by the river, to touch the water and listen to her singing. We do not have to work hard. We do not have to think and try to figure things out. What we need to do is feel. When we feel, we are happy."

Then he invited us to lie down on the ground. "This is an invitation," he said. "I am not telling you that you must, but perhaps you would like to?" Taita Haskusht picked up the small drum and stood up. Everyone moved to the ground, some sitting and some lying down.

I lay on my back in the grass. It was a warm, sunlit morning, and the earth beneath me felt comforting. Above, branches of lacy, green leaves danced in the wind. They reminded me of the leaves on the locust trees back home. Beyond the branches, white clouds rose and flowed in the air currents. I could smell the grass and feel the soft air touching me. I closed my eyes as Haskusht began to drum softly.

"Feel every breath," he told us in Spanish. Then he began to chant in Kichwa, "*Waira, waira mama za.*" Haskusht moved about us in a circle, chanting and drumming. He circled slowly, as a large bird floating in the sky might.

A voice in my mind said, "Breathe deeply; savor every second of this experience. Feel. Feel." I heard occasional sighs from others who were lying nearby. I began to drift.

Taita Haskusht flowed over each person, pausing to blow a whistling wind across us. Then all was quiet. Suddenly, an Andean flute soared and a shaker rattled, while a drum reverberated through our circle. My drifting attention took shape. In my mind's eye, I saw a lime-green spiral spinning. It was a flickering, snake-like shape that undulated and wavered in my inner vision, moving in time with the rhythm of flute and drum until my identity merged with the movement, and I *became* the green spiral slowly spinning above the ground.

After a time, I settled back into my body. I felt the earth beneath me and the cool movement of air around me. The sounds of flute and drum again pierced my awareness.

When I opened my eyes, almost everyone was sitting up, looking at the musicians who seemed to have appeared out of nowhere. Three young men, dressed in white with long black hair tied in colorful ribbons, stood smiling at us, holding their instruments—drums, flutes, and shakers. In the collars of their tunics, a single, colored string was woven at the neck—one wore orange and the others blue. I would later learn that these colors represented the individual's age. The musicians were laughing, and we were clapping. The Condor and the Eagle had met.

We shared lunch together under the trees—potatoes with a warm, salty sauce made from the seeds of squash, lentils cooked with cilantro, chunks of fresh cucumbers and tomatoes mixed together and salted. After lunch, we gathered in a circle again under the pepper tree where Haskusht's father and grandfather had also sat years ago to tell stories and teach.

Now Taita Haskusht told us the story of the training of the musicians.

> Few musicians in Ecuador are trained any longer in the ways of the iachak. Yes, there are many folk musicians. They are accomplished in the melodies and rhythms of the people. They know the lyrics of the songs. They know how to entertain in the markets. But they do not know the iachak way of music, which is the way of ceremony and healing.
>
> Some years ago, my three friends here came to me and asked if I would train them in the ways of the ancient musicians. They wished

to learn how to heal with music. I agreed to teach them. I told them, "You must come live with me."

They came to live with me and my family. They brought their flutes and shakers and drums. I told them, "Put your instruments away. Let us work in the fields." They worked all day for many days, helping the families in this community. At times we went up into the mountains to the sacred waterfalls for purifications and initiations. They gathered plants with the Mama Iachaks and learned the plants' names and their healing properties. At night, they would ask, "When will we play our instruments?"

Maybe my young friends who wanted to learn more were not happy with me? The crops they had planted were ready for harvest, so we had to bring in the harvest. And, of course, the animals needed care and the children, so they helped there too.

At night, we sat around fires with the community. We told stories. We drank aromatic teas and laughed. And in the morning, perhaps one of my young friends would ask, "Now will we play our instruments?"

You see what I mean? I am not good at planning.

One year passed, then another. The musicians worked and played in the community. They traveled with me to other communities and participated in mingas, helping members of the community with projects that were necessary to the people's survival.* After two years had passed, my young friends no longer asked when they were going to play their instruments. They no longer thought about it or wondered. They were filled with the light of the people and the power of the plants and animals. Then, one morning, as the sun was rising, I called them to come do the morning salutations. We stood in the rising light of the sun, greeting Taita Inti.† When the ceremony was complete, I

---

*Minga is Kichwa for a community work-fest. The word emphasizes Taita Alberto's teaching that we learn by doing together.
†Taita Inti is Kichwa for Father Sun.

said, "Now it is time. It is time for you to play your instruments."

But when my young friends went to the places where they had stored their instruments, they were broken and moldy, and no melody or rhythm could be found there.

"You must make new instruments," I told them. "You are new. Your bodies, your hearts, and your minds are new. Your instruments will be as new as you are."

So the brothers went to the rivers and cut canes and reeds. They collected seedpods and dried gourds for their shakers. They found agave cactus that had died and took the hollow trunks for their drums. In ceremony, they sacrificed a goat for the skins of the drums. When the instruments were complete, we took them high into the mountains and left them for three days in the open where the sunlight, the wind, the rain, and the moonlight could enter them. If, when the instruments were retrieved from the mountain, their sound was sweet and true, if they had survived the elements, then they would be instruments of healing, instruments of power.

And now, you see, these musicians are more than musicians; they are iachaks too.

After the storytelling, Taita Haskusht suggested that we take time for solitude, for walking where we wished to walk or for resting. "When the sun is setting, we will share the gifts of the mother together," he said, referring to the evening meal. Then rising from his seat, Haskusht turned and walked away.

I spent the afternoon sitting near the family's small vegetable garden behind the house. The air was cool. I had a wool shawl with me, and as I was sitting in the shade, I pulled it around me for warmth. Bees buzzed in the nearby flowers, and occasionally, a brilliantly colored hummingbird hovered close by. I could hear a rooster crowing in the distance, dogs barking, and mingled laughter and conversation as the family and the musicians visited in the nearby house.

The *chacra* (or family garden) was not planted in rows but in circles and mounds. Some of the plants were known to me, but others were unfamiliar. Corn, beans, squash, potatoes, and peas predominated along with kale and lettuces intermingled with radishes, cucumbers that trailed along the ground, and huge bushes of tomatoes. A tall, reddish plant that dominated areas of the garden was quinoa, the fabled ancient grain of the Andes. This was the first time I had seen it.

Though the garden may have appeared disorderly to those accustomed to the linear gardens in the States, it was actually planted with a deep, inner sense of order and purpose. I had learned something of these ways of growing food from reading about the traditional ways of planting in the Anishinaabe communities of my area in Michigan. The arrangement of the plants provides mutual nourishment as beans, for example, fix nitrogen, which the corn would otherwise diminish in the soil. In addition, the tall stalk of the corn or, in the case of the Kichwa garden, the quinoa, provides a sturdy pole for the beans to climb. Large-leaved plants like the squashes provide shelter from the high-altitude intensity of sunlight for the smaller, more fragile plants and aid in moisture retention in the soil that direct sunlight would evaporate.

Gazing at the vibrant corn and companion plants in this little family garden, I felt close to wisdom. The cornstalk nearest me caught my attention. The wind rose, moving the stalk so that it swayed back and forth in front of my vision. I stood up and walked up to the corn and touched it, being aware as I did so of its presence. This individual stalk of corn was taller than I. It carried at least a dozen ears, partially grown.

As I stood there, feeling the soft breeze and touching the corn, I heard myself wondering, "Why am I here?" I did not feel as if I were asking a question that required an answer; it was more of an open spaciousness to which I needed to attune my attention. I was in a dreamy state, simply feeling the gentle air and the companionship of the corn.

I returned to the shady spot where I had been sitting, picked up my journal, and drew a picture of the corn. Beneath the picture, without forethought, I wrote one word: *sing*. I did not know what this meant, but I knew the meaning would come clear in time.

That evening, the women of Taita Haskusht's community prepared a lovely meal of the same foods we had shared in the morning—sweet blackberry soup, fresh cheese, and soft bread purchased at the market. After sunset, we gathered in the large meeting room that Taita Haskusht had built for his guests to watch a presentation of traditional dances. There was no fire in the room, and once the sun had dropped behind the mountains, the air became cold. We wrapped ourselves in coats and blankets and sat in quiet anticipation as the musicians prepared their instruments. The dancers were preparing themselves in the kitchen next to the meeting room where we could not see them.

As the drums began a quiet rhythmic beat, four dancers, dressed in white, emerged from the kitchen doorway and stood in a line—an older man, two young men, and a young boy. Then in the kitchen doorway, a maiden appeared. With shiny, coal-black hair and face serene, sweet, and dignified, she was dressed in a purple skirt and white blouse embroidered with multicolored flowers. Her shimmering black hair was pulled back and held in a long pony tail by a yellow ribbon wound round and round and round, almost the full length of the pony tail. Tiny gold earrings dangled from her ears. She wore a black shawl about her shoulders and loops of gold necklaces at her throat. Her shoes were white—a flat sole, topped by cloth with a squared toe-piece and white ribbons that tied the shoes to her ankles.

She stepped into the room, carrying a small basket. She moved toward the men one step at a time. With each step, she paused, twisted gracefully, first to the left, and placed the basket on her left hip; then with the next step, she twisted to the right and placed the basket on her right hip. She continued this gesture, with each step transferring the basket from hip to hip, while a soft drum accompanied her. Then three more dancers emerged through the doorway, an older woman, and two young girls. Each was dressed similarly to the first dancer, though in different colors—black, white, or red skirts with black, white, or red shawls—and soft blouses covered with flowers. Each wore gold necklaces and earrings, and each carried a basket. As each dancer emerged from the kitchen doorway, she joined in the rhythmic movement, timing her steps precisely with the dancer before her, placing the basket with quiet attention from hip to hip. As they moved toward the men, who were standing quietly, waiting, the dancers' steps were soft, soft, slow, slow, and careful. There was no hurry. The dancers stepped with dignity and grace; the sound of their white shoes on the red square bricks of the floor, a quiet tapping.

An immense depth was communicated in this slow, ritual dance— the feminine approaching the masculine. The women being the movement, like Air, Water, and Fire; the men being the unmoving, stable, and fixed Earth.

Gradually, the women and the men came together, and then as they paired by age, they formed a circle and began to move, first clockwise, then counterclockwise, first very slowly, then more rapidly. Now the flute joined the drum, and the volume of the music grew. As the dancers moved more rapidly, they seemed to become one fluid, whirling ribbon of color—another image and feeling of snake greeting my eyes. As they gradually slowed their pace, each dancer became distinct again, a separate being, returning to simple, quiet steps, each foot placed carefully and quietly. The flute grew quiet; the drum slowed. And the dancers stood still.

There was a hush in the room, a breathless quiet. Entranced, we visitors were momentarily as still as the dancers, and then, as if on a single exhale, we all began to clap. The dancers bowed to us and then made their way back to the kitchen followed by the musicians.

Within moments, the lights in the room flickered and then failed. Taking this as a signal, we quietly rose to go to our beds to sleep under small mountains of blankets.

THREE
THE LOVING EARTH

THE NEXT DAY WAS MARKET DAY in Salcedo. We rode in a colorful bus, painted various shades of red and yellow. The bus was small compared to the buses I was accustomed to in the States and not new by any means, but it had an elegance about it that was enchanting, with seats of black corduroy trimmed with red leather, arm rests capped with chrome, and foot rests that could be adjusted for comfort with a lever at the side of the seat. With window latches jingling like bells, we made our way, bumping and swaying, through the countryside to the city, listening to music on the bus radio—a version of the then-popular theme song, "My Heart Will Go On" from the movie *Titanic* played entirely on Andean flute.

The only graffiti on the bus was one English word etched into the back of the seat before me, so that I gazed at it as we rode along the rural roads: *love*.

In Salcedo, the open-air market was noisy and crowded. In a central square under a roofed pavilion with a cement floor, vendors had set up booths or were displaying their wares on blankets on the ground around the pavilion's perimeter. Scarves woven of bright green, purple, and turquoise were draped above the tables. Hand-sewn cotton blouses embroidered with delicate flowers and nightgowns woven of unbleached cotton were displayed on hangers. The tables were laden with mounds of lettuce, kale, cabbage and broccoli; carefully stacked cucumbers; thick bunches of cilantro; pyramids of bright, red tomatoes; and baskets of strawberries, grapes, bananas, mangoes, papayas, and other fruits that were new to me—*uvillas* and *granadillas*. On the floor were large woven sacks of quinoa or maize; red, yellow, and green peppers; ears of corn with plump, white kernels; and white and purple potatoes.

We threaded our way, single file, past women dressed in black skirts and white blouses with lace at the collars and necklaces of gold beads. The women wore colorful red, bright blue, or black shawls; some wore blue aprons. They stood near the tables or sat on the floor near their baskets of lush foods and looked up at us as we walked past. A few extended hands full of dried beans or rice. Young women nursed their babies or watched their children playing nearby. Men dressed in traditional clothing—white pants and shirts, long, wool ponchos, and fedora hats—stood in small groups, talking among themselves.

We had come to visit a Mama Iachak who was held in high regard by the local Kichwa community for her knowledge of herbal medicine. The herb woman sold many plants that she and her family had gathered from remote mountain areas. She was small, perhaps four and a half feet tall. She wore a bright blue shawl around her shoulders and a black felt bowler hat. She stood inside a square formed by four waist-high tables. Each table was piled high with vibrant, green plants—so green and moist they seemed to have been picked that very instant.

Our translator, Sara, told us that if we had any physical ailments, we could ask the herb woman which plants would help. One traveler had a sore throat. Sara translated the English into Spanish to Taita Haskhusht who then translated the Spanish into Kichwa to convey the information to the herb woman. Quickly, she selected individual plants, her hands moving deftly among the piles of green, putting together a bundle of four or five different plants, which she then tied together with a thin vine. I recognized some of the plants—borage, lemon balm, and pansies. Others were unfamiliar to me. Each of us received a bundle of plants from the herb woman; even those who had not requested any were given a selection of plants, determined by Haskusht's and the herb woman's assessment as they looked at us.

When we finished at the herb woman's stall, Taita Haskusht led us through the market, back under the roof, and out the other side, stopping where two young girls were selling spices packaged in small plastic bags. The spice bags were clustered in a basket on the ground at our feet. Haskusht stopped and told us that these spices—peppercorns, anise, cinnamon, and cloves—were good for bathing. Sara translated Haskusht's words: "For purification, the aromas lift the spirit. Soaking in the spices helps cleanse the body." We purchased the girls' entire basket. Haskusht seemed delighted.

Later that afternoon, back at Haskusht's home, we sat in a circle in the meeting room, each of us holding the bundle of plants we were given by the herb woman. Sara sat beside him to translate, and Haskusht began to teach us about the plants. He told us their names in Spanish and in Kichwa. He told us their uses. Then he reminded us to follow our hearts in choosing which plants our own bodies need. "Perhaps you think you need to read in a book to learn all the uses of a certain plant," he said, looking about the circle. "But what you need to do is feel with your heart what it is that you need. Trust what you feel. Perhaps what you need is not in the book. You may find even that you do not need to take a lot of a certain plant. It may not be necessary for you to steep large quantities of the plant for many hours. Perhaps all you need is one tiny leaf. Or perhaps you do not need to ingest the plant at all. You may only need to touch the blossom, or inhale the fragrance, or look at the plant's shape and colors. You may simply need to sit beside the plant for an afternoon or a day, or to return to it for many days. You may only require subtle contact."

The next day, Taita Haskusht, Sara, and several young people from the community took us on a walk to an area where in the 1950s and '60s logging interests had completely denuded the slopes of trees. Haskusht explained that the village once occupied these lower Andean ridges, but when the trees were taken, erosion forced the village to move to the lower plain where it is now. We walked past small holdings—houses where a pig or cow was tethered by a rope and where garden areas were crowded with vibrant plants.

As we walked, our guides stopped to talk with their neighbors, rarely introducing us but simply exchanging local news and laughter. It was almost as if, to the Kichwa, we visitors were invisible, not actually there. They did not appear to look at us or to be in the least curious about us. Perhaps Taita Haskusht's feeling was that our presence was something of an intrusion and that introducing and acknowledging us would make it more so. Perhaps it was simply that we were irrelevant to the conversations that he was having with his neighbors. Whatever the reason, there was little open acknowledgment of our presence as we walked with him. Certainly, the community was keenly aware of the visitors, and as I would learn in later years, to some at least, our presence was not desirable.*

As we walked, Haskusht invited us to select an individual plant and to take some of it with us during the walk. "If you see a plant that calls you," he said, "you can pick some of it."

A ground cover plant that grew along the roadside attracted my attention. Its small, deep-green leaves were formed in half-moons, and its tiny flowers were a soft shade of lavender. I paused and gazed at the plant, then knelt close to it for a time while Haskusht helped other members of the group who were asking him the names and uses of plants they were attracted to. Before picking the plant, I paused, remembering

------

*Haskusht would later tell me that there was considerable controversy in his community and in other Kichwa communities whenever visitors from Europe or North America were present. The communities had firsthand experience for many generations of disruption, deception, and destruction caused by non-Indigenous peoples. They had little reason to trust that this would change simply because Taita Haskusht was attempting to educate these foreigners.

Rolling Thunder's teaching that we should talk to the plants, that we should tell them what we will use them for, and if we are using them for medicine, that we should say why we are seeking healing and how we plan to use the health that is given to us.[1]

I touched the tiny leaves. "For medicine," I said within myself, directing the thought to the plant. "For healing," I added. "To shed a skin if necessary," I heard myself whisper. "To be of service," I said aloud. I took a small frond of the plant, perhaps two inches in length with a few small blossoms and put the flower in a button hole of my shirt.

Standing up, with the tiny plant near my heart, I walked forward toward Haskusht who had moved farther down the road and was walking with Sara and several others.

When I caught up with Taita Haskusht, I asked Sara to translate for me. Up to this point, I had not asked Haskusht any questions. I was absorbing so much that I did not feel any impulse to speak. A great deal of information and experience was coming to me directly. I felt that it wasn't necessary to ask questions, that anything I needed to know would come to me. Haskusht stopped walking and turned toward me. I touched the plant in my lapel and asked its name. Before Sara could translate my words, Haskusht put his hand over my mouth and turned away. Surprised and hurt, I stood still in the road while Haskusht and the others continued walking. I felt heat in my body and face, a flush rising from deep within me, as I recognized the intensity of the wound that had been triggered. A woman in a garden some distance from where I was standing, stopped hoeing and looked up at me. The moment that she raised her head and glanced at me, her dog charged toward me and started barking angrily. I turned my back, hoping that if I ignored the dog, it would consider its job accomplished, and walked hurriedly to catch up with the group.

I joined the others, and gradually, we climbed the slope behind the village until we arrived at an area where there were no houses, some cultivated fields, but mostly a barren expanse of dry, ashen-gray, cracked soil, the visible result of the logging that had happened almost fifty years ago. Here Haskusht had organized a community effort to replant trees. For about three miles along the base of the slope, just above the village, hundreds of saplings were visible, most only a foot or two tall.

Rafael, one of our guides, told us that his family had watered many of them when they were first planted, carrying drums of water up the slope and then dipping smaller pails into the large drums and distributing the water to each tree individually. "We dream that our grandchildren will sit in the shade of these trees. We dream that these trees will bring the water back," he said.

Rafael's comment reminded me of the Buddhist concept of "mutual arising," the understanding that nothing exists independent of other beings, that everything arises in conjunction with everything else. When Rafael said that the trees would bring the water, I understood him to mean it literally—the more roots, the more deeply they work their way into the earth, and the more water they will call for the trees and the surrounding land.

After witnessing the infant forest growing along the slopes, we continued our walk until we came to a crevice in the earth—a deep cut, the base and sides of which were carpeted with the same plant I now wore in my lapel. Haskusht invited us to sit in the midst of the thick, green plant-life dotted with tiny lavender blossoms. Now the plant I had chosen—or more properly, that had chosen me—surrounded us, its tiny form woven into soft mats beneath us, springing up in gentle flowers beside us and wafting soft aromas above us. We were cradled in green plant life and lavender blossoms close to the earth.

The sun was very bright. As I moved to sit, I noticed a disturbance in my vision. Within seconds, I realized that I was seeing a migraine aura, something I was familiar with from having had occasional migraines in the past. First, I saw a bright, spinning light which quickly resolved into a row of zigzagging triangles fringed with green edges moving in a rapid circle at the center of my vision. I felt momentary panic, realizing from past experience how disorienting a migraine could be. Dimly, I heard Taita Haskusht inviting us to lie down on the earth, to connect with Ashpamama.*

I lay down and closed my eyes as the migraine aura increased in vividness and intensity. Then Haskusht began to chant a low, melodic call, sweet and strong.

In the past, when experiencing a migraine aura, it would inevitably be followed by severe headache and nausea, but as I lay on the ground, a clear instruction came into my awareness to "follow" the aura instead of fighting it. So I calmed my fear by simply paying attention to the spinning light. As I listened, Taita Haskusht's chant wove itself into the rapid movement of the aura, both sound and vision circling and flowing. Now into my awareness came long-forgotten memories that I associated with being silenced.

A wave of emotion surfaced, and I felt a sudden flow of tears that seemed ancient and overwhelming. I heard an inner voice speaking, "Give the pain to the Earth." But I resisted, thinking the pain was so great that the Earth would be harmed. But the voice reassured me, "I am the Mother. Release your pain in me, and I will transform it."

Now, before me, in my inner vision, the green triangles became golden and seemed to be painted into clay. I recognized flowing designs circling a Navajo vase—a beautiful vase, the vessel of life. And then above me I heard sudden, loud flapping, the wings of some huge bird, rising up out of the grass, released.

After a time, Taita Haskusht's chanting ceased. I heard the woman next to me crying. When she and I sat up, she explained to me that she had been overwhelmed by the grief of her father's recent death and that

---

*I often hear non-Kichwa people speak of Pachamama as Mother Earth. Taita Haskusht always emphasized that Pachamama is the Great Cosmic Mother, a force larger than planet Earth, whereas Ashpamama in Kichwa refers specifically to Earth itself, as does Allpamama.

she, too, had been called to release the pain into Earth. We hugged each other, sharing comfort and quiet.

When everyone was ready, we began our walk back to Haskusht's home. I felt weak, shaky and drained, but the vision disturbance had disappeared and no headache or nausea followed. By the time we reached Haskusht's home, my strength had returned.

Back at Taita Haskusht's home, we gathered in a circle. Haskusht came over and sat beside me, touching the plant still in the lapel of my shirt. He said, "*Esta planta cura la voz. Nos ayuda a hablar nuestros sueños. Nos ayuda a hacer realidad nuestros sueños. Esto nos permite cantar,*" and he smiled at me. Realizing that I did not understand him, he called Sara to come over and translate. He repeated his words, touching my throat, while Sara translated, "This plant heals the voice. It helps us speak our dreams. It helps us make our dreams come true. This makes it possible for us to sing."

After our circle, we all rested until dinner. We gathered again after the sun had set to share a meal, one of the most profound gifts that I received at Haskusht's home.

"Eating is the greatest ritual of all," Taita Haskusht told us, "because this is when we commune with the Mother. When we eat, we are receiving the love that Mother Earth is giving to us. We must feel the love of the Mother," he added. "This love is transformed into Earth through colors, through aromas, through flavors. Mother Earth did this for her children. She did this with love for many months, and we are her children—her sons and daughters—and we need to be grateful for this."

The food, which the women prepared with love and care, was medicine to us. The meals they made were exceptionally delicious and created a feeling of strength in my body, clarity in my mind, and calm in my emotions.

That night, we again slept close to the earth on simple mattresses placed on the floor, covered with layers of heavy, hand-woven wool blankets. I rested near an open window where chamomile scented the night air, while soft breezes rattled tree branches against the roof and moonlight illuminated the quiet room. But even though brilliant moonlight shone through the little window above my bed and even though many creatures were awake and busy, I fell into a deep, tranquil sleep.

FOUR
THE SACRED RIVER

MIDWEEK, TAITA HASKUSHT TOOK US to a hot springs for a purification ceremony. To immerse ourselves in warm water, we had to travel many miles by bus to a public hot springs. After an hour or so of traveling, we arrived at an open, wild landscape where several shallow, cement-lined pools had been created to funnel volcano-heated water upward. There were no visitors other than ourselves and a few wandering sheep.

Taita Haskusht invited us to pause at the edge of the pool and before entering the water, to first look about us—to see the foothills rising around us, to see the sky that on this day was brilliant sunlight, to see the scarce vegetation and the dark, pebbled earth. "*Simplemente mira*," he said, "*y siente qué es lo que te gustaría expresar.*" (Simply look and feel what it is that you would like to express.)

Then he called us to kneel down at the edge of the pool and touch the water gently. "It is important to feel the water," Haskusht said. "Before you enter, pause and greet the water. Caress the water. Feel the water touching you; feel what it gives to you. Share with the water; share your thoughts and emotions. Your heart will feel a response, and then you will be moved to express gratitude to the water. It is very natural. You do not need to work at this. Let the water teach you to flow. This is a very special ceremony."

After perhaps half an hour of quietly kneeling or sitting at the edge of the pool, Haskusht invited each person to step carefully into the water. Slowly, we immersed ourselves in the intense heat. Some sighed, some murmured. Taita Haskusht entered the water with us, not speaking, and stood, waist high, looking outward toward the hills. For a long time, while people floated or soaked, Haskusht stood in an attitude of reverence in the same way that a heron will stand motionless in shallow water, attending, with a quality of patience that is far greater than that of those who watch.

After the necessary time had passed, Haskusht climbed out and called each of us to emerge slowly and follow him barefoot across the gravelly ground. We walked in the cool mountain air to an icy stream, perhaps two hundred meters from the springs. The stream was shallow and lined with rocks. "Lie down here; in this stream. Lie down on your back and feel," Haskusht said, motioning to the bright, shallow water rippling briskly across shiny pebbles and rocks.

Still warm from the hot springs, I lay down, my body soft and fluid compared to the hard, mineralized rocks beneath me, but the icy cold of the water was an intense shock. Unable to remain in the river for more than a few seconds, I sat up almost as soon as I had lain down and jumped out of the water. Others were able to stay in longer. Taita Haskusht did not enter the river at all.

Standing beside the river, I felt a current of energy rush through my body, vitalizing every cell. I was shivering as I made my way quickly back to my pile of clothes and wrapped myself in a sweater. My mind felt brilliantly awake and clear; my body was shaking with the cold. I lay flat down on the ground to be free of the air currents and to receive the sunlight as completely as possible.

After a time, everyone came back from the river. The members of Taita Haskusht's community who had come to the hot springs with us went to the bus for a moment and returned carrying thermoses. They poured each of us a cup of hot chamomile tea.

Haskusht spoke to us while we sat drinking the soothing liquid, wrapped in towels and blankets. He reminded us that everything that enters our mouths enters the rivers in our bodies.

"We have to remember when we honor water to honor the water that is inside us as well," he said. "Think of how most of our body is water. Yes, the waterfall or the rain is wonderful, but in our bodies is the wonderful water too. Yes, we want to clean the rivers on the planet. But we must also clean the rivers inside our bodies. When we clean the rivers inside our bodies, we are strengthened and made clear so that we know how to clean the rivers that are outside us on the planet. I know people who are very concerned about the environment; they fight and protest and want laws to make the rivers clean. But these same people do not take care of the rivers in their own bodies. Sometimes what they drink poisons their own rivers. They do this because they have lost the ability to feel, so they do not notice."

Then Taita Haskusht told us a story of his early childhood. "When I was very young, before I could even walk, my father, who was a Taita Iachak, would carry me in his arms to the river. We would go to the river where no other people were, so we could be alone with the water. My father would dip me in the water and say, 'See the little children in the water. You can play with these children in the water.' And then I would see them, in the small drops of water, many children playing and laughing. But there were no people there, only my father and myself."

Sitting beside the river at the hot springs, Taita Haskusht spoke to us of the iachak path—the path to wisdom. "Here you are learning to feel. When we learn to feel the water—both outside and inside our bodies—then our physical body becomes activated in the right way, and this allows our other senses to be activated too. That activation allows us to feel the other worlds. If a person doesn't eat right or lives a life that is very unorganized and unbalanced, the senses will start to shut off. But when we connect in the right way with the elements, it affects us on a cellular level. It is a molecular vibration, and then we become able to fly in many worlds because our senses are awakened to the many different realities. We can do this by learning to feel.

At any moment we want, we can achieve a state of great happiness because using our five senses and awakening our other senses in a natural way brings us into deep connection with the Great Force of Life. In my language, Kichwa, we call this great force Jatun Pachakamak. This great force that is Life is not outside us; it is not way up there in the sky. It is here, within us, in this moment. It is everywhere. It is everything. When we feel this great force flowing through our bodies, flowing through our minds, flowing through our hearts, we have experienced a very great purification and a very great truth."

In the late afternoon, we returned to Taita Haskusht's home. He asked us to not eat anything for the rest of the day, to only drink chamomile tea. A large pot of mildly warm water was placed on a table in the large meeting room with a ladle and cups beside it. Fronds of chamomile floated in the pot and sent a sweet aroma into the air. Some people went quietly to their rooms to rest; others gathered on the grass outside the house to converse. We went to sleep early that night, our bodies still releasing impurities as a result of our hot-springs and cold-river baths and our fasting.

In the night, dogs barked in the distance, and music played until dawn. I felt restless and uneasy. I was sleeping in a room with six other people, both men and women. I awoke numerous times. Late in the night, I awoke suddenly, feeling strong fear, and looked quickly to the steps that led into our room. I was certain that I had heard footsteps, and it seemed that in the dark I could make out the movement of head and shoulders coming up the steps, but I could not see clearly. The room remained quiet, and I convinced myself that I was imagining.

In the morning at breakfast, we learned that Sara had been very ill during the night. Taita Haskusht explained that Sara would not translate for us that day, but one of our members knew enough Spanish to translate for him. "There was a great battle in the night," he said. "Sara wanted to know why no one came to help her. My family was there beside her, but Sara could not see them. No one else could help her because we were all engaged in battles of our own. I went up into the mountains, to a sacred place, and there I closed the gate."

Taita Haskusht then asked us to tell him what we had dreamed during the night. Many stories were shared—some straightforward, others not easy to decipher. After a long conversation, Haskusht said, "Yesterday, we did the purification. We soaked in the hot springs; we rested in the river. We did not eat, so our bodies could rest and cleanse. In the night, these impurities were able to rise up and take shape. They were leaving, and maybe some of us could see them as they were leaving. When this happens, when these energies are rising, we can hear them or see them or taste them. Then our emotions become very strong. So you need to keep your mind still. It is not helpful to interpret what you are seeing or hearing or feeling. You do not need to tell yourself stories. It is not helpful to be afraid. It is necessary simply to be very quiet, and the energy will leave you in peace. This is a very great test that happens when we purify. The imbalances that are leaving—maybe they would like to stay with us longer. Maybe, even, we would like them to stay with us, so we think about them. We look at them; we talk to them. This is not so helpful. This is the mind not being willing to let go. We must talk to the mind. We can say to the mind, 'It is OK. You do not need this any longer,' because we must let go if the purification is to be complete."

Then Taita Haskusht lit a candle that was close to him and placed a thin stick of wood into the flame. The wood caught fire. Haskusht allowed it to burn until the flame transformed into smoke. The smoke gave a sweet aroma. Haskusht brought the smoking stick of aromatic wood close to each person, wafting the smoke around them. "This is *palo santo*," he said, "a very beautiful, sacred plant. It loves us very much."*

---

*The aromatic wood comes from a tree (*Bursera graveolens*) that grows in the semiarid areas of coastal Ecuador. The wood has been used by the Kichwa for generations as a healing agent. Its aroma is sweet, and inhaling it lifts the mind into sweetness.

When he had finished smudging each person with the palo santo, Taita Haskusht said, "We will stay here today. Tomorrow, Florentina will take you to the river to wash your clothes, but today we will stay close."

◇◇◇

On washing day, Florentina, a young woman in Haskusht's community, invited the women in our group to come with her to the river to wash clothes, if we wished, and to do ceremony. It was early morning, about two hours past sunrise. We had broken our fast of the day before with papaya juice only, and now we walked with small bundles of clothes down the dirt path that led behind the house to the river. Sara was feeling much better, and she came with us to enjoy the washing and to translate for Florentina. We walked past fields of maize and quinoa, small herds of llamas, houses where barefoot children played in the yard. Along the sides of the path, agave cactus rose many feet above our heads.

Florentina stopped by one of the agave. Because it had rained earlier, small pools of rainwater had gathered at the base of the cactus where two stalks met. Florentina dipped her hand into the water, bringing a small amount to her mouth. Speaking Spanish, with Sara translating, she told us, "This is medicine—the most powerful medicine. When the rain sits in the agave, this medicine cures the heart. If we are sad, if someone we love is far away, this water helps." She invited each of us to dip our hands in and taste the water. It was cool and pungent, refreshing. We murmured our gratitude, and it did seem as we walked along with Florentina that my heart lifted. How wonderful to be here in this beautiful place, walking with a small group of women, as women have walked for centuries, smiling in the early morning sun, carrying our washing, feet bare on the earth, plant water coursing through our veins. Any remnants of tension left over from the purification seemed to lift and float away.

When we arrived at the river, we put down our bundles. We stood where the bank sloped gradually to the river. Before this point and after it, the water rushed over rocks, but here, there was a small pool where the current had slowed. Florentina stepped into the water and began to sing. She dipped her middle finger into the water and touched her forehead with the water. Then she turned, clockwise, to each direction—north, east, south, west. She sang while touching the water, then touched her wet fingers to her forehead—once for each direction. Because she sang in Kichwa, we did not understand the words she was singing, but we could feel reverence in the way she touched the water and in the way she touched herself. Her motions were gentle and quiet, her face serene. All about us, the many beings joined her song. The water rippled and gurgled across the rocks. The breeze fluttered leaves and branches that seemed to click in rhythm with Florentina. Tiny birds hopped from the tree branches onto the rocks close to us, dipping their beaks into the water, drinking, and then flying up to the tree branches to sing.

One by one, we each stepped into the water, and in our own ways, we greeted the water and felt its cool, murmuring embrace, gratitude welling up naturally in expressions of laughter and song. Soon, we were all singing to the river, and the river was singing to us.

Then we moved to the bank and sat down together. Some of the women in our group now began to share stories, stories of sadness and alienation that they felt in their home countries. Some of the stories were wrenchingly painful, and as each woman who spoke described her sadness or confusion, Florentina, who did not understand the English, listened intently. Sara did not translate, for it appeared that Florentina did not need to understand the English words because she was listening to the emotions that were being expressed. She seemed to understand the emotions clearly.

After each woman spoke, Florentina motioned the woman to sit upon a large boulder in the river. For each woman, as she sat there feeling the wet cold of the rock and the radiant warmth of the sun,

Florentina gathered fronds of certain plants that grew close to the water. She held the plants in one hand and brushed the woman sitting on the rock with the plants, beginning at the top of her head and moving through her whole body down to the feet. After each long stroke, she shook the plants toward the water, not touching the water, but vigorously shaking the plants. Florentina turned her head to the side often during the cleansing and coughed repeatedly as she brushed the woman and shook the plants. This process continued for some time, while the rest of us sat on the shore quietly watching. When finished, Florentina took the bundle of plants and placed them on the ground in the sun.

All morning, we sat by the river, some of us washing clothes, some of us resting on the bank, some of us speaking quietly together. When it was time to head up to the house for lunch, Florentina spoke again and Sara translated: "Whenever you are lost, come to the river. Sing to the river. Tell the river that you are lost. The river will lead you home."

FIVE

THE SPEAKING WIND

WE CANNOT FORGET THE WIND while in the Andes, where movements of air create continual change in the atmosphere. Clouds are thick one moment, and the sun is brilliant the next. For a time it rains, then rainbows appear, arching from mountain peak to mountain peak. The constant movement overhead is echoed in the movements of trees, shrubs, and plants and in the travels the people make every day, walking from home to village or field, sorting, carrying, sharing necessities, working in the fields, resting when the sun is high, preparing food, spinning yarn, weaving cloth, making music, dancing, and singing. With the wind flowing shadow and sunlight over animals—wild and domestic—with birds soaring and alighting, the air communicates with perpetual motion.

Most of our time was spent at elevations above eight thousand feet. For those of us who had come from sea level, shortness of breath made us aware of the air and of our lungs. It was harder to walk rapidly than at home; we had to inhale more deeply and rest more often. Loads felt heavier and sometimes emotions arose unexpectedly. Taita Haskusht reminded us to greet the air when we were out of breath, to experience the oxygen entering our bodies with all of our senses, to express gratitude for the life-giving breath exhaled by the plants around us.

We experienced the heightened sensitivity brought on by cultivating our awareness more deeply on the day we traveled up Cotopaxi. As solid and Earth born as the mountains are, they are also beings of air, surrounded by clouds, circled by hawks and, here, the rarely-seen Condor. Ecuador's portion of the Andean chain includes many active volcanoes. This volcanic activity emphasizes the way the elements always intermingle—fire deep in the Earth spewing forth liquid rock, steam, and smoke. The exhalations of air from within Cotopaxi's core—visible in the sky above as soft, snake-like plumes of light—warn of the intense activity hidden below and communicate the proximity of sudden and dramatic change.

Taita Haskusht spoke of Cotopaxi as his great teacher and guide—and seemed especially happy to be taking us to this sacred place.

We traveled by bus, wending our way along the narrow roads that circle Cotopaxi, rising higher and higher into the air as we traveled. The road wound gradually up the mountain, climbing until we reached a plateau at about thirteen thousand feet where there was a place to park. Here a small lake called Limpiopungo, which means "cleansed-point," was our destination.

We climbed out of the bus into wintry-cold air. Wind whipped my cape into my face and slapped it around behind me. Thin slivers of rain blew through the air, and above us, clouds streamed rapidly across the sky. Even though the air was full of movement, the lake water was steely gray and still. The shore was volcanic gravel, black and rough to the touch, the vegetation sparse.

No longer was Cotopaxi distant. No longer did we sit in the protected, green yard of Haskusht's home, gazing at the cloud-hidden peak. Now we stood more than halfway up Cotopaxi's side. At thirteen thousand feet, another six thousand feet of volcano towered above us, rising in dark majesty above the lake.

Taita Haskusht, in poncho and fedora, stood very still; the wind was blowing even stronger now. Sara stood beside him, wrapping her shawl more tightly about her. Haskusht turned to look at Cotopaxi's cone rising behind him. As he gazed at the cloud-wrapped mountain peak, the cone of Cotopaxi emerged from the clouds. Haskusht smiled and spoke. Sara translated, "To see Cotopaxi's face is rare! This is a great gift. The mountain is greeting us."

Gazing at the mountain, I felt an almost grim quality and recalled cruel Caradhras of the Tolkien legend. But even as I had this thought, I realized how little I knew of this mountain. I reminded myself that words like *grim* and *cruel* only said something about me, about my response to the mountain, about the way I was "dreaming up" Cotopaxi.* So I asked myself to listen.

Taita Haskusht invited us to follow him to the lake, to greet the Earth at the shoreline, and then to greet the dark water that seemed motionless, largely undisturbed by the currents of air. It seemed that the water had such depth and was so cold that even this strong wind was unable to agitate it.

With the wind blowing at our backs, Sara stood close to Haskusht and translated: "We must express gratitude to Madre Waira, to Mother Wind," said Haskusht. "We must permit the air to take away our dark thoughts, to take away our infirmities, to take away the negative things—the sadness—all the heaviness that we have in our lives. This is a gift that the air gives us—to lift up—to take away all of the things that we do not want in our minds, in our hearts, in our lives. We must permit the air to give us the gift of transparency, of health, of intelligence, of positive ideas, and we must express gratitude for all these gifts of health, of blessing, of love and prosperity."

As he was speaking, the wind again rose. Sara's shawl lifted up and

---

Dreaming up is a term coined by Arnold Mindell, creator of process psychology, referring to the way all human beings project their personal stories onto the world.

blew away from her body. Haskusht snatched it just before it blew into the water and returned it to her, laughing, "*Ah muy muy poderoso!*" he said. "Very powerful. The air is inviting Sara to fly. The air is asking each of us to fly higher and higher, to fly inside our dreams, to fly so that our dreams may materialize in our lives, so that everything we wish for—harmony, peace, health—may come to us. We fly so that the air may bring us these gifts."

"You can sit here now," said Taita Haskusht. "Sit at the feet of Cotopaxi and feel." As we sat down, the sun broke through the clouds, the rain stopped, and the wind quieted. Haskusht stood, gazing at the lake for a time, while everyone settled into the bare earth, some seeking shelter inside a curve of the bank that rose to the path, others huddling near the weathered, rough shrubs.

I pulled my hood over my head, drew my knees up to my chest, and rested my forehead on my knees. I was hidden inside my black cape, surprised by how effectively it diffused the power of the wind that was buffeting again but was unable to loosen the folds of the cape because I was sitting on it firmly. After a time, I felt the presence of Cotopaxi seeping into my body.

Soon I was dreaming. Words began traveling through me: "Whatever happens, don't look up. Whatever happens, don't look back." I did not question the message; I listened to it as to a chant. I assented to the command, "OK, I won't look up. I won't look back. No matter what happens." The chant resonating in me caused me to recall the fairy tales in which trust demands that the hero or heroine not look at something or not turn to look behind at the path they have walked. I recalled Orpheus turning back to his beloved Eurydice and so losing her; Psyche lighting her lamp and looking upon the lover she had been warned she should never see. Fearing him to be a monster, she is compelled to look. Discovering him to be Cupid or Eros, the ideal expression of Venusian love, she is, nonetheless, forever banished from his companionship as a penalty for having looked—for having succumbed to her fear.

Always, the fairy tales call the attention forward: "Do not look back! Do not look back!"

The wind tugging at my cape brought me back to my present condition. For a moment, I thought I heard bells and someone breathing beside me. I almost pushed my hood back to look, then remembered the chant, "Do not look . . . do not look." I brought my attention to the heat flowing from my body, warming the inside of the tent I had created with my cape. My hands touched the gritty earth I was sitting on. With my left hand, I scooped up a portion of the mountain soil. I let it sift through my fingers.

Then, quietly, inside myself, I greeted the mountain. I said, "Hello. I see you. I am here with you," and then I spoke the name, "Cotopaxi." Hard ground, cold wind. Though my eyes were closed, I was aware of shapes and presences around me, their forms shrouded in various shades of slate gray and black. A feeling of elemental origin—a time or condition before color, before form—enveloped me.

Again, I spoke the name, "Cotopaxi." Now I felt myself to be entirely alone, walking in a cylindrical corridor of energy. There was no wind, no rain, no lake, no companions, only silence and the feeling of walking.

Time passed, but I was moving outside time. As sensory input disappeared, the mountain presence grew. I felt an awake consciousness emanating from Cotopaxi. I recognized an immense being, far beyond anything I knew, far beyond any parameters or storied dreams that my mind could tell or my words express. I sensed that this presence, this Cotopaxi, was not indifferent to us. I sensed, even, that assistance was available here, and in that moment, I felt awe and, more deeply than ever before, the need to be in right relationship, to feel with my whole being genuine, sacred respect for the mountain and for the beloved Earth.

After a time, I heard rustling and felt movement as everyone (it seemed it must be everyone, though I was still buried in my cape and could not see) stood up and moved off toward the bus. I lifted my hood and looked up. Immediately, the feeling of connection to the mountain faded. "Do not look up!" I had forgotten the command. I put my head back on my knees, disappointed in myself, not ready to leave. I felt I wanted to give something to Cotopaxi. I reached into the small medicine pouch that I kept in my pocket and felt there a smooth, triangular stone—an Apache tear, as it is called in the States—that had been given to me by a young Cherokee Blackfoot man from Arkansas who had, through the oddest of circumstances, ended up on my dirt road in Michigan one early summer day, holding a dying snake by the tail.

Two days previous, this young gentleman and I had had a powerful meeting. As a result, he had contacted his mother who was a medicine person on a reservation in Arkansas, and she had instructed him to bring me the Apache tear. On his way to my house, he had discovered the injured snake in the road. That snake and I knew something about each other, and that stone had given me great assistance since that time. It had been a teacher, a very great helper to me. At times in the past when I feared that I had lost the stone, I had felt panic. Now I wondered if I could let it go.

I took the stone out of my pouch and kissed it. Then I put it under a bush that was near me. For a time, I watched the stone. After a while it seemed too visible so I gave it a little push, and it rolled out of sight. I took a deep breath and placed my hands flat on the ground beside me. Under my left hand, the heart hand, I felt a hard lump. At first I did not pay any attention to it. I was gazing at the lake and thinking I should move. Then I noticed the rough sensation under my hand. I withdrew my gaze from the lake and turned to look at what I was feeling. It was a small chunk of volcanic rock shaped just like the Apache tear—only instead of the smooth, silky feel of the polished Apache stone, this rock was mottled and rough to the touch. I picked it up and put it into my pouch.

When I rose to leave, I saw Taita Haskusht, his poncho moving in the wind, looking at me, with cloud-hidden Cotopaxi behind him. He waited for me as I walked toward the bus. When I reached the place where he was standing, he said, "*Si, es verdad: vivir en el pasado no sirve.*" (Yes, it is true: to live in the past does not serve.)

Coming down the mountain, we took a different route than the road we had traveled upward. We seemed to wind downward, downward, downward in a gradually-widening spiral until we came into a verdant, lush valley, where a cascade of water fell from a high cliff down the mountain toward the road. Here the bus pulled to the side of the road, and Haskusht invited us to walk for a time.

At this lower altitude, the air was cool but soft. I Inhaled deeply of the mountain air, feeling the intensity of the life force it offered. Steep slopes of patchwork fields and pastureland where sheep grazed rose on both sides of us as we walked along a narrow path. Small huts of those who lived here seemed to emerge out of mist. I wondered about the life here, where there was no electricity, possibly no clocks, and no town just around the bend. What did they think, I wondered, of the occasional bus or car that went whizzing past? Was this mountain home their entire experience? Or did they, too, find a ride—a way into the city, into commerce, into the busy, noisy world? A part of me—perhaps the heart that was loosening some of its defenses—yearned in that moment to live in a small dwelling amidst waterfalls, green fields, and rocky mountain walls. With bits of wood fencing to keep the animals in; a pile of wood cut for the fire; black, tilled earth, and a stream, I, too, could rise early, work in the fields and tend the animals and garden.

I considered the many generations, the hundreds of years—indeed! the thousands of years—that my ancestors, agricultural peoples, had lived where the only sounds were wind, water, fire, and birds, animals or people calling.

This mountain crevice seemed a place outside of time, a place where time had never existed. Here, it was only sun or rain, light or dark—season upon season; and those who lived here, all that happened here, forever held within the large presence of Cotopaxi.

SIX

THE FIRE
OF HAPPINESS

ONE EVENING NEAR THE END of our visit, Taita Haskusht gathered us indoors. It was chilly, and we were all wearing jackets or ponchos. Haskusht sat at one end of our elliptical circle beside a small potbellied stove into which he periodically put a twig or fan of leaves. Mild warmth issued from the stove, but not enough heat to warm the large room we were sitting in. The room had many windows, and above the windows, there were gaps large enough to admit birds who flew in and out under the tiled roof throughout the day.

Haskusht lit a short stick of palo santo in the fire. The tip of the stick caught fire; a bright flame flared as Haskusht pulled the stick out of the fire. After a few moments, the flame transformed into aromatic smoke. The palo santo sent a sweet aroma throughout the circle while Haskusht spoke. Sara sat beside him, translating. Haskusht looked around the circle and asked in Spanish, "How are you feeling?"

Only a few of us answered the question directly, but a single comment from any one seemed to express worlds. Haskusht listened intently, often making no comment after one of us had spoken. It seemed that he was listening deeply both to the person's words and to the atmosphere that surrounded those words.

After a time, he said, "I am very happy to see you all here." He paused. A log shifted in the fire and sent a few sparks into the circle. "We have been together before," he continued, though he was not referring to previous visits but to previous lifetimes.

"We are now together again. We agreed to come back at this time to be together. You bring the gifts of the Eagle to the South. Here in the South, you are learning the gifts of the Condor. The Eagle is very good with the mind. You are gifted with intellect, technological know-how, and financial prosperity. The Condor lives from the heart but sometimes forgets to make plans, to work for the future. The Condor can learn this from the Eagle. The Condor needs help with technology and science. The Eagle needs help listening to the heart. We need both gifts—both the mind and the heart—for balance."

"It is time now for us to join together," Taita Haskusht continued. "It is time for the Eagle and the Condor to fly in the same sky. Five hundred years ago, the prophecies said this time would come. And you see?" laughed Haskusht. "The prophecy is true because here you are." We laughed in response.

Someone asked, "Haskusht can you tell us about that time long ago? What happened then?"

Taita Haskusht was quiet. Then he said, "The elders knew then, more than five hundred years ago, that there would be a long period of struggle. It was no longer safe to do the practices. Outsiders came and said, 'Oh, you are worshipping the sun. That is a bad thing.' But we were saluting the new day, giving thanks for the many gifts, receiving the breath of Jatun Pachakamak, the Great Force of Life. There was a long period when these things were not understood."

He stopped speaking and put a branch into the small fire in the stove. He was looking at his hands and at the burning branch, not at us. We were very still; even the fire stopped crackling. I wondered if Haskusht was recalling painful memories. I sensed that he did not want to say everything that he knew.

Finally, he looked up and said, "But it is safe now. It is time now. The elders have said that we can share the teachings now. It is time to be very happy."

Then Taita Haskusht told us of his father's death. "We were very close," he said. "We spent a lot of time together. He was my teacher. Whenever he traveled, I went with him. Then one day he said he would be taking a trip soon, but that this time I could not accompany him. I did not understand what he meant. I thought, 'OK, I will not go with him on this trip, but then he will return, and we will continue to go on trips together.' Then, one day, I noticed he was walking two inches above the ground. I thought, 'Oh, that is interesting.' Four hours later, he collapsed. I held him in my arms, and I started calling him, bringing him back. I did not want him to leave me. But then I realized it was his time to go, and I let him go. In the days following his death, I went around arranging the things that needed to be arranged. I felt I was flying. People could not understand why I was not in grief. They were surprised that I was happy in the days after his death. But, you see, I could feel his heart even though I could no longer touch his body. I knew he was continuing his journey. I knew he was very happy, so I was happy too."

Haskusht paused. The palo santo smoke had ceased. Again, he held the tip of the stick in the fire; again, the stick caught fire and flared as he brought it out of the fire, burning for a bit, then transforming into sweet smoke.

Haskusht looked at us intently. "Remember, we are not our bodies. We are that which gives life to our bodies. That which we are continues when our bodies are no more."

As I looked around the circle at the members of our newly forming community, I saw tears in some and quiet thoughtfulness in others. I recognized my fellow travelers in the world of spirit and felt deep respect for each person sitting there. I could see two aspects of everyone in this moment. I saw their personality, the nuances and difficulties that happen at the personality level, and I also saw the sincerity—the soul-level intention and hopefulness—of each person there. No one had come to Haskusht's home by accident. No one had come who was not willing at a soul level. And the surface inflections of personality, though necessary and part of the work for each of us, were still not the determining features of our destinies. It was what each of us had chosen at a soul level that was emerging through us now.

Taita Haskusht's words brought me back. "I will be with you for a little while," he was saying. "If you want me to, I will walk with you. Whatever game you would like to play, we can play. But remember, when I leave my body, please be very happy. It is a wonderful thing to fly between worlds. This is what you are learning here," he continued. "You are learning to fly. The fire will help you; it will help you feel. Fire activates our love for one another." Then he stood up, motioning with his arms for us to rise and saying, "Now we can dance."

Because the night was cold, Taita Haskusht invited us to drum and dance to warm ourselves. I walked away from the group toward the table where the large pot held warm chamomile tea. I ladled up a cup for myself, and as I turned from the table, I turned into Haskusht who had walked up behind me. He placed his hands gently on my arms and kissed me on the forehead.

The sound of the Andean flute rose above the mingled voices in the room. The musicians from Otavalo were with us. They called everyone to make a circle. One drummed; another played the flute; another played the pan pipes while shaking a rattle made of sheep's hooves. I moved forward into the group and took the hands of my new friends. Someone called for Haskusht to join the circle, but he had disappeared.

SEVEN

TIMELESSNESS

IN ECUADOR, TIME, FOR ME, was not marked. Roosters crowed all night; people in the village near Taita Haskusht's home played music, danced, and partied until an hour before sunrise. When I stirred in my sleep, I heard drums, rhythm, and wind. The sun rose quietly and quickly behind purple hills and set as quietly and quickly behind similarly purple hills. I felt, while there, both that time had elongated and that time had evaporated. What existed instead of time was wind and seed, rain and fire. I never felt hurried. I felt as if all time was available to me. Nor did I feel, while in the midst of beauty, that a time would come when I would have to leave. Though I knew in my rational mind that I was only there for a brief period and that, indeed, the end of that period would come, the ending never seemed near. The concept of a week or a month—a chunk of demarcated time with boundaries around it—lost meaning. This way of conceptualizing simply was no longer relevant. Everything was breath. Everything was present moment.

It was at Pasochoa that the sense of deep eternity intensified in me. Pasochoa, a national preserve south of Quito, is a cloud forest, so called because during the rainy season mist envelops the trees, and one feels that one is walking through clouds. We visited during the dry season, so there was no mist. Indeed, the landscape felt not unlike a sunny wood in North America, though bamboo grows in abundance there as do hallucinogenic mushrooms and tropical plants whose blossoms are so tiny they could be easily overlooked in the thick, green overgrowth.

The forest begins at about nine thousand feet in altitude. Those wishing to climb higher into the *páramo*—an alpine tundra ecosystem—will ascend to almost thirteen thousand feet. The paths are strewn with silky leaves of bamboo. At the lower altitudes, most of the path is a gradual incline, though some areas are steep and slippery. Sunlight, filtered through the green canopy, illuminates lush orchids trailing languidly from the trees. Birds of radiant plumage, like the hillstar with its cap of lapis lazuli blue, flit rapidly and call, only occasionally seen. The air is rich with the scents of moist earth and plant life, and it is quiet—if, by quiet, one means only the sounds of wind, plants, and creatures are heard. Deep in the forest, only the forest speaks; there are no sounds of human machinery. Here is where the puma finds security.

Small waterfalls and rushing streams border the path, and in unexpected moments, the traveler comes upon secluded pools where the water is cold but not icy. Sitting by such a pool, immersing oneself in the water, years of forgetting are washed away. One awakens, only now realizing the difference between living and sleepwalking.

The final day of our visit, we were at Pasochoa morning, noon, and early afternoon. Yet, even though we walked for the morning, lunched in a sunny field, and dozed in thick, deep clover afterward, time did not seem to pass. That night I would be flying home, but no thoughts of leaving entered my mind.

At one point during the morning walk, I happened to be walking next to Taita Haskusht. People were behind us and people were in front of us, but for a time, he and I were the only two, walking beside each other on the path. As we walked, I looked down at the path we were walking, and there I noticed four legs, moving rhythmically, walking . . . just walking.

As we walked, Haskusht paused and turned to look directly at me. I, too, paused. *"Eres una mariposa,"* he said. (You are a butterfly.) Then we resumed our walking. The forest around us seemed hushed and gentle; the silvery bamboo leaves beneath our feet made soft, silky sounds. I was taken, suddenly, by a deep sense of how eternally Haskusht and I are walking beside each other. There was no emotional coloring to this awareness, nor were there many thoughts. I simply experienced visually and in the energetic feel of Haskusht's body beside mine the keen understanding of what it means that four legs are walking the path—always, always, and the awareness that many share this path.

What I heard as Taita Haskusht walked beside me was: "Eternity. Eternity. There is no time. All there is, is the path. We are always walking, and we are always together."

At Pasochoa, we experienced a closing ceremony, lying on the ground high in the mountains, while raptors flew overhead. We rested in a meadow of thick, spongy grasses that had never been cut by any blade, reaching their own, native height before tumbling over each other and intertwining to create the thick mattress that supported us.

Taita Haskusht walked among us, drumming slowly and softly, occasionally emitting a brief, high-pitched whistle. "Hold your heart's desire in your mind," we heard him say. I visualized a world made sweet by love expressed and children fed, a world where terror is not only emptied of power but has become its opposite. Lying there, I encountered with precise clarity and no emotional evasion the ways in which I had interfered with and had turned away from this possible world. I saw the terrain of my own imperfect life, mapped and revealed to the inner eye. I saw what I had been creating with my fear and my desire. I saw the story I had been telling. "The story you tell is the story that happens," chant the medicine people.[1]

Midafternoon, leaving Pasochoa for the ride back to Quito, we rode a narrow dirt trail barely wide enough for the small Latacunga bus. In order to go around occasional deep holes or large boulders, it seemed that the bus must somehow make itself smaller, and I had the feeling that, indeed, the bus was capable of contracting when necessary, that we were squeezing through the tunnel of trees and rock face that bordered the narrow road.

Above the bus, thick vegetation grew so low to the path that it scraped the windows as we bumped our way along, dipping suddenly to one side or other, jerking forward, then halting and moments later lurching forward again. The windows were open, and bamboo and eucalyptus branches whipped past us, scraping along the rim of the windows, shedding leaves into our laps. The aroma of eucalyptus wafted through the bus on a dry breeze. Andean music, a flute and much singing, rolled from the bus radio, accompanying the laughter and storytelling of the people riding there. I was sitting beside Taita Haskusht, gazing out the window.

I turned from the window. "It seems like a dream," I said to Haskusht in my faltering Spanish.

"Todo *es un sueño*," Haskusht replied. (*Everything* is a dream.)

We arrived in Quito as the sun was setting. The noise and pace of city life were pressing. We taxied to the airport where we assembled in the small lobby with our bags, preparing to say goodbye to the community members who had helped us get to the airport and to express our thanks to them and to Taita Haskusht. Though we had paid lodging, board, and tuition to Haskusht, we did not feel that this in any way adequately paid for what we had received. Some in the group were tearful at the parting; some ecstatic at what they had experienced.

Haskusht smiled and encouraged us. "In my language," he said, "in Kichwa, there is no word for goodbye. This is because nothing ends. Our souls will continue to meet."

I was leaning against a wall, wearing a white wool jacket, handmade by the Kichwa, my suitcase on the floor in front of me, waiting for the long line ahead of me to pass through the turnstile. Haskusht worked his way through the crowd, came up to me, and hugged me. I remembered his words, the night we sat with him before the fire. "As you take on this work," he had said that night, "you will encounter many tests.

These tests will be very difficult. And when you pass one, there will be another one, and it will be more difficult than the one before." I had listened then, knowing the truth of his words. "But," he had added, "you will not be given a test that you are not ready for. You will not be given a test that is too difficult for you. And remember," he paused, waiting while we all looked at him, "I will always be with you."

PART TWO

BECOMING
A RUNA

Purification and
Sacred Communion

EIGHT

THE PATH
OF THE RUNA

THE KICHWA REFER TO PEOPLE who are deeply connected to the Earth as *root people*—those who are planted in the earth, whose roots draw sustenance from fertile depths. "We have a root," said Taita Alberto, "A cosmic root, a historic root, a cultural root, a mystical root. We are beings who come with a very special potential. We must again connect with our roots, with the forces of the cosmos, to have clarity in our lives, to know our direction."[1]

Characteristic of root people is reverence for the Earth and for all of life. The rooted live with an open heart. In Kichwa traditional teachings, *heart* is defined not as emotions but as the innate capacity to *feel* one's connection with all of life. If the heart is open, the heart is receptive to subtle energy streams, and thereby, the human being knows, instinctively, how to be a member of the Earth community. The person moves *with* Nature's flow, not against it, walking their life path in the way a jaguar walks in the forest. Heart-connected, the human is certain that they belong in the natural world.

If heart is feeling connection with all of life, what is *mind*? Mind is intellect and reason. Intellect gathers and retains information, while reason makes connections among the various data that the intellect has stored. Contemporary science and technology are examples of mind. When mind works in concert with heart, scientific and technological advances contribute to the well-being of all beings.

When heart is activated, a person understands that Nature is their teacher. When heart is activated, a person pays attention to the various impulses that come from the natural world through their five senses. Each sense offers different and vital information. When a person directs their attention to a specific sense—for example, asking, What do I smell on the wind?—the mind receives information that the reason can then apply to make wise decisions. This alert, sensory, and intuitive capacity enables a heart-connected person to live in rapport with the natural world. When mind is aligned with heart, they are able to follow Nature's teachings. And because Nature is supremely wise about how to perpetuate life, when they follow her flow, they are better able to perpetuate life.

Not following Nature's flow is to live *unrooted*. When one is unrooted, balance is lost. The person cannot feel the earth beneath their feet, and there are no roots to anchor them. As a result, the mind becomes confused. Intellect and reason—the positive capacities of mind—become submerged beneath ego fears and desires. In this state, the priorities of the unrooted sacrifice health and well-being for the short-term salving of fear and the short-term gratification of desire. When governmental structures, public policy, and corporate interests are equally unrooted and unbalanced, the whole ethic of a culture moves in the direction of harm, and all of life is threatened. The result is that the once-positive capacities of mind—intellect and reason—are now made servants of the impulse to dominate, to control, and to win at all costs. Separated from heart, separated from the ability to feel kinship with other beings and to know their responsibility to the Earth, the unrooted wander with no genuine sense of direction.

Many live every day with no awareness that they belong to the Earth. Uprooted, they may not feel any sense of belonging. We know that, beginning in the early twenty-first century, many people became more familiar with loneliness, alienation, and grief than with companionship, inclusion, and comfort. Some are suspicious of anyone they do not identify as being like themself. Many experience deep levels of fear and dread; for if one does not belong on Earth, if one does not belong in the cosmos, where is safety to be found?

In Kichwa, the word *runa* describes a person who is walking the path of life in a sacred way. To be a runa is to live a life of beauty and harmony. A runa is filled with the joy of dawn, the potency of plant life, the freedom of bird flight, and the creative flow of the river. To be filled in this way is to feel that heightened condition of intimate belonging in the natural world that was known to our ancestors. This is what the Kichwa elders hope we will return to—that ancient way of being fully connected to all of life.

A runa establishes this connection through participating in the universal conversation that is happening around us all the time. An essential characteristic of participation is the capacity to listen. Through respectfully listening, the human being hears the natural rhythm and learns again to *be* that natural rhythm, which is their birthright. The result is a rekindling of the human being's experience of belonging in the world, of belonging to the Earth and to the cosmos, and the ultimate effect is an awakening of happiness and joy—the opening of the heart. And, in Taita Alberto's words, when we again connect with our cosmic roots, we harmonize ourselves, and as a result, "we contribute to the harmonization of the world."[2]

Taita Alberto invited us to reenter conversation with the other beings who share our world, a conversation that at one time would have been innate for all of our ancestors. Over centuries, the Western tradition gradually rejected this communal and integrated way of relating to the natural world. In his book *Dream of the Earth*, Thomas Berry refers to the loss of the ability to participate in the universal conversation as a version of autism in which the one stricken knows only how to converse with their own kind. The consequence, Berry writes, is that "the experience of sacred communion with the earth has disappeared."[3]

With the Industrial Revolution and the movement of many people into cities and away from daily, intimate contact with the land, many on Earth neglected this ancient conversation to the degree that what we now call the "modern" world—what Taita Alberto called the "world of the city"—has entirely forgotten the ancient bond that humans once had with other species.

Healing this form of autism, what we could call "Nature-autism," was Taita Alberto's path. His own relationship with the natural world was so intimate and so pure that simply being in his presence conveyed the feeling-state of intimate communion with the Earth.

To restore that ancient bond, Taita Alberto taught reconnecting with the elements—Earth, Air, Water, and Fire—through actively conversing with these powerful energies. In *The Fruitful Darkness,* Joan Halifax asks these essential questions:

> Will we talk to mountains and clouds, I ask myself, as our ancestors did? Will we ask the oak whether we should plant a garden near it? Can we hear the voice of the stones in the sweat lodge? Can we hear salmon asking us to protect and restore their rivers? Do we understand what owl tells us in the dark of night, or what the clouds say in their silent script? Can we hear the sounds of the world, like Kuan-yin, the Buddhist goddess of compassion?[4]

Those of us who journeyed with Taita Alberto were invited to enter this ancient conversation that, at one time, all our ancestors practiced. Taita Alberto sought to elicit a natural and spontaneous playfulness in his students, encouraging us to relax, to trust, and to enjoy. He spoke of these practices as "forms of expression from the heart that many people call rituals," but he emphasized that it was important to not do the practices mechanically, step by step, but to do what we feel in the moment.[5] That said, Taita Alberto did offer three steps for conversation that are described below to help those who are new to this type of encounter to know where to begin.

To teach this way of conversation, Taita Alberto invited us to meet each of the elements as a being. He often reminded us that these beings are very great, so great that the life of our human body depends upon them. No Earth, no human life. No Air, no human life. No Water, no human life. No sunlight, no human life.

In the Andean mystical tradition, the elements are recognized as beings who are immense, conscious, and intimately involved in our lives. To the mystic, Earth, Air, Water, and Fire are deeply aware of us. And, Taita Alberto would emphasize, not only are they aware of us, they are also willing—in fact eager and waiting—to help us. This does not mean, however, that these beings are "thinking" in the sense that the previous sentence may seem to imply.

NOT ANTHROPOMORPHIZING

Newcomers to these practices, if trained in a contemporary, industrialized-culture attitude, often feel resistance—either consciously or unconsciously—to conversing with a tree, a rock, a mountain, a lake, and so on. This is because they assume that the invitation to converse implies an assumption that the tree, rock, mountain, or lake is conscious in the same way that a human being is conscious; and they resist this idea. They have been taught not to anthropomorphize.

To anthropomorphize is to project human characteristics onto the forest, the wind, the rain, or the sun. When a person is anthropomorphizing, they may say, "The wind is angry," or "The tree told me to take a hike." They are either consciously or unconsciously assuming that the element they are encountering is thinking like a human, and thus, when they have thoughts and insights or feel emotions, they may attribute these experiences to the being that they are paying attention to.

It is fairly easy to discern when a person is anthropomorphizing because, often, they will relate a very detailed story, such as one I heard years ago at one of Taita Alberto's workshops in the States. A member of the workshop told us that they had discovered that the shrubs in their yard were jealous of one another because they had given one of them a "haircut," as they called their pruning, but not the other. The individual was highly entertained by their own story and detailed the petty jealousy evinced by members of their hedge. That is anthropomorphizing—human ego entertaining itself—and to do that entirely disrupts the possible depth and expansion that can happen in a genuine encounter with another being.

Taita Alberto was *not* inviting students to anthropomorphize. Rather, he was inviting and modeling a sacred practice during which the human being lets go of their ego, their fear and desire, in order to encounter, with full respect and unbiased openness, another being—a presence that exists in this world with them but is not embodied in human form and, thus, expresses its own, highly-individualized nature.

As we know from classical meditation practice, human ego interferes with the potential of full, awakened presence. A sacred conversation is not a "device" for the aims of the human ego—a pretense of reverence that masks the human's attempt to get what they want. No, genuine encounter happens when all ego attachments are put aside, and the person becomes present, as will be described more fully below in the discussion of feeling. With full, awakened presence, an encounter between two beings is not impaired by any "dreaming up," to use Arnold Mindell's phrasing, of the nature of the other.[6]

What *is* the "true" nature of tree, for example? Can a human being sit quietly and not expect something from that tree, not want a teaching or guidance or help of some sort, but instead just be present at the same time that the tree is present? What is that experience like? And might there be a teaching in that experience that comes not because one has attempted to get it, but because one has stopped trying to get anything and has simply become still in the presence of the tree?

The nature of the consciousness of other beings can feel familiar to us because all beings share the cosmic field, but we cannot define, take hold of, or put parameters around the nature of the consciousness of these large forces. They are too immense for our tiny boxes. Their nature is beyond the comprehension of the human intellect and reason. However, while we cannot intellectually contain precise knowledge of these great forces, we can *experience* these great forces throughout our whole being. Our body, our mind, our emotions, and our spirit all sense the energetic presence and information available when experiencing intimate contact with the elements.

To feel our connection with Earth, Air, Water, and Fire is to feel our primal reality. It is to realize the deep perception, present in all mystical traditions, that, as Taita Alberto often said, "We have different appearances, but our essence is the same." A cat, a tree, a house, a person—all share a fundamental essence, the Ushai.

Taita Alberto spoke of Ushai as the fifth element. Ushai is not static; it is not something that is parceled out equally to all humans for example. Rather, Ushai is a spiritual force that can be diminished or expanded depending on a person's way of life.

As Taita Alberto expresses in his book *Friendship with the Elements*: "Every activity or *ruray* [rite] that we perform with the intention of harmony, well-being, love, solidarity, reciprocity, complimentarity—enlivens, grows our Ushai, and that in turn, grows our *sumak alli kausai*—our life of happiness, harmony, plenitude, clarity, well-being."[7]

When the four elements—Earth, Air, Water, and Fire—are in balance within a person, then their Ushai is enabled to grow. The practices described below are intended to help a person expand their Ushai by helping them harmonize the four elements within their being.

Taita Alberto told his apprentices that the Ushai was not often spoken of by his elders. He said there was a feeling of such great power in the Ushai that the elders were cautious about speaking the word. But

Taita Alberto felt that in these times it was important for people to understand the reality of this force, to realize the influence of Ushai, and to know that their thoughts, words, and deeds had a direct effect on their own Ushai and on the Ushai of others.

The cosmology of the mystical traditions of the Andes teaches that Ushai manifests in a potentially infinite variety of forms, appearing in various physical manifestations and then disappearing. Beings are always emerging from and returning to the Ushai, a field of pure potential.

In the mystical practices, the individual begins to perceive from the perspective of the field. When perceiving from the perspective of the field, what appeared to be other is now revealed as oneself. *Tat tvam asi* (thou art that) chants the Hindu tradition. *En lak esh* (you are the other me) chants the Mayan tradition. "When you are happy, I am happy," Taita Alberto would say.

The practices described below initiate us into primal identification with all of Nature—an experience of undifferentiated wholeness in which the individual experiences themself as being both a part and the "whole." It is a condition that has been felt by mystics and articulated by poets for thousands of years. The Persian poet Rumi hints at this condition:

> *We began as mineral.*
> *We emerged into plant life*
> *and into animal state and being human,*
> *and always*
> *we have forgotten our former states*
> *except in early spring*
> *when we dimly recall*
> *being green again.*[8]

It is a condition evoked in an early Irish poem attributed to the legendary Druid bard Amergin:

> *I am the wind which breathes upon the sea*
> *. . . I am a beam of sun*
> *. . . I am the fairest of plants,*
> *. . . I am the wild boar in valour*[9]

It is a condition that many feel in early childhood if fortunate enough to be left to wander freely outdoors—a condition that the English poet Wordsworth sought to recapture:

> *There was a time when meadow, grove, and*
> *Stream,*
> *The earth, and every common sight,*
> *To me did seem*
> *Appareled in celestial light,*
> *The glory and the freshness of a dream.*[10]

It is a condition that nineteenth-century philosophers and poets in France, England, and America, with their wistful, anxious, backward gaze toward their own grandparents' time, sought to name and recapture in the face of the Industrial Revolution and the depredations that their own colonialism had wrought in the land and in Indigenous peoples.

The transformation invited by the practices that Taita Alberto teaches is a transformation that arises through cultivation of the capacity to feel, mystically, this union that we have with all beings. "*No es teoria*," Taita Alberto would say. It is not theoretical. It is actual. When we enter sacred communion, we experience our original nature—our wholeness—a condition that Taita Alberto would refer to as "*un ser humano completamente realizado*," a fully realized human being.

Taita Alberto spoke of "*un extasis permanente*"—a permanent ecstasy—that a person who fully integrates the practices into their daily life will experience, an ecstasy that does not fade over time. This ecstasy does not fade because it is not dependent upon anything external to the individual person.

For example, this ecstasy is not dependent upon ingesting a plant helper. Within the general field of shamanism, sacred plant teachers are often used. However, the practices I was taught did not include the use of coca, datura, ayahuasca, or other psychoactive plant preparations. There is a reason for this. As Taita Alberto has said regarding power plants:

In order to respect these plants and all of Pachamama, one should not use them without great need. Power plants were and are used when a person with sufficient serious preparation and discipline has not been able to feel any connection with a part of the great spirit of life. . . . [Power plants were/are used] as an emergency measure, as a final recourse with care, mental and emotional preparation, [with] a physical cleansing and with direction and supervision from a Jatun Taita Iachak or ancient shaman, who would administer the drink in an exact dose designed specifically for that person. [It is not done] as they do now, that every interested tourist is offered shamanic journeys without sufficient time for preparation in any aspect.[11]

Regarding entheogenic (god-filled) experiences, ultimately the teaching is that *all of Nature is entheogenic*. The original condition of the human being was effortless participation in the sacred dimension of being. To remember that all of Nature is entheogenic is to recognize that we are innately entheogenic ourselves. When we open the channel of communication between ourselves and the elements, we activate the entheogenic energy that each of us already carries, the divine nature that we all are.

In sacred conversation, the runa learns to move into a condition of open awareness in which the ego, or personal identity, does not shape the experience. In that open condition, the runa travels into sacred time-space, a pacha, that is omnipresent but not always perceived when a person is consumed by ego concerns. The human being both acknowledges their place in the natural flow of life on Earth and *participates* in that natural flow.

RECIPROCITY

In his brilliant essay "Seeing with a Native Eye," Barre Toelken, a folklorist who lived with the Navajo in the 1950s, explains that the Navajo say that when one is ill, in order to be cured, "one needs not only medicine, . . . one needs to reestablish his relationship with the rhythms of Nature." Toelken goes on to explain that the Navajo rain dance is much more profound and complex than the "praying for rain" interpretation that early observers and anthropologists provided. Rather than asking a deity for help, the rain dance is a way of moving that brings the human back into right relationship with the cosmos. The dance is a ceremonial method of aligning oneself and the community with the organic rhythms of nature. When the human moves in concert with Nature, they are not interfering with the natural rhythms. Not only does their movement invite the natural rhythm to return, they also will not be moving in a way that impedes the rain. Writes Toelken:

> I have had Pueblo people tell me that what they are doing when they participate in rain dances or fertility dances is not asking help from the sky; rather, they are doing something which they characterize as a hemisphere which is brought together in conjunction with another hemisphere. It is a participation in a kind of interaction which I can only characterize as sacred reciprocation. It is a sense that everything always goes this way. We are always interacting, and if we refuse to interact, or if some taboo action has caused a break in this interaction, then disease or calamity comes about. It is assumed that

reciprocation is the order of things, and so we will expect it to keep appearing in all forms."[12]

We could say, to build on Toelken's phrasing, that to stop conversing with the other beings who share our world amounts to a *refusal* of our sacred responsibility to participate consciously in the cosmos. We compound the wounding caused by this refusal when we add to it the tabooed action of manipulating Nature in an attempt to impose human will without considering the effects our actions will have on the other beings who share our world. These are the behaviors of one who is very ill. When such behavior is replicated ad infinitum by almost all members of a culture, that culture is on the brink of self-imposed annihilation.

So it is that elders in many Indigenous cultures are reaching out to the unrooted—to offer them medicine, to offer them healing, before it is too late.[13]

It is possible to hear Nature's rhythm and to know how to follow that rhythm. Not only is it possible, it is essential if we are to survive as a species. While this may, at first, seem to be a difficult task, it must be remembered that rootedness is our original nature. It is our own natural way of being that we are learning to recover. The way of sacred communion is not foreign to us; it is just forgotten.

It is possible to learn again how to speak with one's relations. To learn the way of sacred communion, Taita Alberto invited his students to do three things: to cleanse their body, to cleanse their mind, and to begin a conversation with the four elements: Earth, Water, Air, and Fire, as these elements present themselves in the person's daily life.

What, then, are the practices that we can do every day, in any time and in any place, to help us return to Earth? How can we return to the feeling-state that was the birthright of our ancestors?

NINE

PURIFICATION AND THE FOUR ELEMENTS

MANY TRADITIONS INCLUDE methods of purification to help a person let go of what is no longer needed and to prepare the body, mind, emotions, and spirit to receive healing energy. Taita Alberto emphasized the importance of cleansing both the body and the mind as ways of transforming a person's inner state to open them to the healing energy around and within them.

In purification practice, Taita Alberto encouraged temperance—not going to extremes. He often said, "No one is ahead. No one is behind. Everyone is precisely where they need to be in order to learn what they need to learn." Fasting, for example, is done gently and not for many days. This demonstrates a basic teaching of Taita Alberto—that it is not healthy to force or to strain. Attempting to force oneself with internal pressure, which usually includes negative thought patterns, is likely to do more harm than good.

How, then, do we approach practice? Is there a sense in which we apply discipline and, if so, how? Notice that the word *discipline* contains the word *disciple*. What is a disciple? A disciple is a person who follows a teacher or a principle out of love. It is love that calls them forward, not force, toward that ideal represented by the teacher or articulated in the principle. If we take the attitude of discipleship when we address changes that we would like to make in our own thoughts, words, and actions, we can feel a sense of being drawn toward something rather than being pushed in some way. When we conceive of these practices as self-love, it is as if our future self who has grown through practice is looking back to us and calling us to follow, to come forward into a more expanded condition. We use the energy of the positive state to encourage ourselves—like the sun attracting the plant to blossom in its direction. This is how we grow in a natural, organic way.

Below, I share some of the techniques of purification that I learned from Taita Alberto. They are very simple, not unusual or exotic, simply clear and peaceful. In part I of this book, I described Taita Alberto's way of bringing those who work with him into a condition that is open to healing. In the Andes, he deliberately brought us into various encounters with each of the elements, without talking to us about what he was doing or about what we "should" learn. He spent very little time during my first journey to Ecuador teaching in the conventional sense. Rather, he simply led us into harmonic relationship with Earth, Air, Water, and Fire, which then encouraged the Ushai to grow.

I have arranged the practices detailed below to follow the pattern of Earth, Air, Water, and Fire, though it is important to note that the elements always intermingle. But in order to make our relationship conscious, it is helpful to separate them while we learn. Each element bears a special, curative relationship with specific aspects of the human being. Taita Alberto taught that consciously interacting with each element is cultivating a friendship with the elements that is available to each person wherever they live.[1]

THE EARTH ELEMENT

The Earth element is our home. It is the physical manifestation through which life operates. The Earth element provides grounding and stability. The Earth element includes all plants and animals, including the human animal. Our body is the Earth element; it is our physical structure, the bones and the flesh that make our life possible. Taita Alberto would often say, "We are Earth walking."

As Earth walking, we need, periodically, to cleanse ourselves to open the channels through which insight and joyfulness flow. As is often said, the body is the vehicle for consciousness, so cleansing the body allows a more pure and perceptive form of consciousness to flow. When William Blake wrote, "If the doors of perception were cleansed every thing would appear . . . as it is, Infinite," he may have been longing for a method.[2] The mystical traditions of the Andes teach such a method. Taking care of the physical body through diet is a first step.

It is common to consider diet in reference to the physical health of the body. We know that our food influences our emotional and intellectual states and that these, in turn, affect how we behave. Food bears a direct effect on how we operate in ordinary reality. What is less understood is that food affects our spiritual life as well. Taita Alberto would sometimes use the word *abertura*, aperture, to refer to the opening—the window, the door, or the threshold—that leads the apprentice into other dimensions of reality. To find this aperture, the channels in the body need to be cleansed, and diet begins that cleansing.

The Iachak Diet

Taita Alberto referred to eating a meal as participating in "the greatest ritual of all," explaining, "This is when we receive the gifts of the Mother [Earth]." As many teachers do, he encouraged us to slow down when we eat, to savor the foods, and to give thanks to whatever life form we are eating. Fruits and vegetable are life-forms, just as animals are. When we eat them, they are giving us their life force. As you will see in the practices below, expressing gratitude is an extremely important part of the ritual of eating.

Even more important than the specific food that is eaten, however, is the person's attitude toward their food. This is a very important point because it is too easy for a person to become judgmental of themself if they eat foods that they do not think of as good for them. This attitude of self-judgment interferes with the digestive process. People are encouraged to enjoy their food, no matter what they are eating, to treat the food with love and respect and to be grateful for the food. This will help the digestion a lot.

The iachak diet, as Taita Alberto taught it during the time I studied with him, was primarily vegan. The families I stayed with during my years of traveling in the Andes were rural people, but not always iachaks. So the family may have consumed animal products, including fish and meat, typically guinea pig.

Dairy, usually cheese, and, occasionally, eggs were given to guests, but at least on the journeys that I experienced, no mammals, fish, or birds were offered to the visitors. The food shared with us was primarily locally grown, much of it from the small garden near the family home. It was common for the families I visited to have their own cow. I did not observe the families using the cow's milk to drink, and Taita Alberto mentioned that milk is not drunk by adults, but it was used to make the light, fresh cheese that was often served with breakfast. Typically, a few hens lived around the houses of the families I visited.

In my experience with Taita Alberto, apprentice iachaks did not consume animal products. When animal products are part of the body's nutrition, it is more difficult for the person to be in an expansive state. An entirely vegan diet begins the cleansing that opens the perception.

However, Taita Alberto would always emphasize that he was not teaching "rules" that had to be followed strictly or unquestioningly. Instead, he would encourage his apprentices to experiment. "See how you feel," he would say. "Do not do this because I say it is good. Do this because you want to know. Because you want to see if you feel different. What you experience—that is the teaching."

During certain ceremonies, even traditional iachaks might consume a small amount of guinea pig, but that is done as part of the ceremony. Related to this, Taita Alberto told me of an experience he had during his training as a iachak. Because he had been reared by traditional iachaks—his mothers* and his father and grandfather—he had never eaten any animal flesh. As part of his training, he was instructed to eat a small amount of certain animals. He said, "As soon as I ate my first bite, I felt the channels beginning to close." The sensitivity and perception that were normal aspects of his state of consciousness began to fade. I asked him, "How long did you feel the channels closed?" I expected that he would answer for an afternoon or perhaps a day or a week.

But he replied, "For about six months." This from only a few mouthfuls of animal flesh.

On another occasion, Taita Alberto was speaking to me about war and violence. "I was asked one time by a general—a person who was in charge of the soldiers that were fighting on the border with Colombia— what diet was best for his troops. I told him that he should feed them a lot of meat. When people eat the flesh of animals, it makes them more violent."

He went on to explain, "When an animal dies in fear, a great deal of adrenaline goes into the flesh. Then when a human being eats this flesh, they are also eating that adrenaline. A person who eats animals is eating the animal's fear. This is one of the reasons I do not eat animals. Besides," he added, "they are our helpers and friends. I do not want my helpers and friends to suffer, so I do not kill them and I do not eat them."

---

*Taita Alberto always spoke of his "three mothers," his biological mother and her two sisters who all cared for him as mothers.

The iachak diet follows a pattern: sweet in the morning, salt midday, sweet again in the evening. Taita Alberto would say, "In this way, we begin and end the day with sweetness."

Breakfast might include fresh papaya or mango juice, bananas, warm grain cereals flavored with fruit and honey, white bread, and herbal teas. The midday meal is the largest meal of the day for the iachak and is the only meal that includes salt. This meal might include a variety of locally grown vegetables, especially potatoes; home-made sauces; simple salads of lettuce, cucumber, and tomato; lentils, salted and flavored primarily with garlic and cilantro; and grains—quinoa (grown locally) or rice purchased in the markets.* Often, the evening meal was comprised of the same foods that were eaten in the morning and included chamomile tea with honey—chamomile from the garden beside the house and honey from the family's hives.

Food Combining

Taita Alberto taught us how to discern the effects of specific foods on the body and on one's energy level. In this practice, a person eats a single food and then waits for a period of time before eating another food in order to sense the food's effect. This helps a person listen to that food and learn how it is affecting them. Often, either the stomach or the colon gives signs of imbalance, or other body symptoms, some quite subtle, may hint at the food's effect. A food will either lift or suppress a person's energy, but many people do not notice this. Eating a single food at a time helps a person discover that food's effect.

A person can determine how a particular food affects them and also improve their digestion by eating foods separately and by becoming aware of how rapidly various foods digest. Fruit, for example, digests rapidly. If fruit is eaten after other foods, it sits in the stomach with

---

*Potatoes originated in the Andes. Taita Alberto said there were about a thousand varieties of edible tubers.

those other foods and, as it decomposes, can ferment, which can result in indigestion. So the suggestion is to eat fruit on an empty stomach and wait half an hour before eating other foods. In addition, waiting a half hour will enable a person to tell whether or not that fruit is compatible by the way the body responds to it.

The following is a general guide for how quickly various foods digest. The times given indicate how long to wait before eating other foods.

1. Fruit: half hour
2. Vegetables: half hour, if juiced, to one hour
3. Nuts and seeds: one hour
4. Grains: one hour
5. Dairy: two hours
6. Eggs: two to two and a half hours
7. Fish: three hours
8. Meat (poultry, beef, pork, and so on): four hours

A person who is vegan is mostly eating foods that move rapidly through the system. Foods that move more slowly are said to putrefy; they tend to become stuck and thereby produce various maladies. That said, however, my personal feeling about this is that it is best for each person to conduct their own experiment, eating foods slowly in the order above to learn how each food has affected them. A person might do this practice for a week or a month and see what they learn.

Then after that week or month of practice, they may wish to rearrange their diet, not necessarily waiting so long between foods, but choosing which foods to include in their diet and which to eliminate based upon how they feel.

Taita Alberto would say that the stomach is like a bowl. Whatever the person eats at the same meal all goes into the same bowl. Those foods are combined in the stomach; during the process of digestion, they have to work together. A good guide, he would say, for determining which foods to eat together is to ask yourself if you would put them all in the same bowl on the table and eat them that way. Would you, for example, put fruit and vegetables and nuts in the same bowl and eat them? Possibly. Would you put eggs, bacon, and toast in the same bowl and then pour orange juice and coffee over them? Possibly not. If a person suffers from indigestion, it may be due to inappropriate combining of foods.

Again, each person can conduct their own experiments with these teachings to see what lessons Nature offers when they pay attention to her messages.

- **Cooling and warming fruits.** Taita Alberto spoke of fruits as having different qualities that are either cooling or warming. When the body is hot and needs to cool, eat fruits with white flesh, such as apples and pears. When the body is cold and needs to warm, eat fruits with yellow, sunshiny flesh, such as mango and papaya.

- **Masculine and feminine parts of the fruit.** Taita Alberto also taught that fruits have a masculine and feminine polarity. The part of the fruit that is attached to the tree, shrub, or plant is the feminine pole; the part of the fruit that is outward into the air is the masculine pole. Women eat from the masculine pole of the fruit. Men eat from the feminine pole.

- **Fasting.** Fasting is common in many spiritual traditions. For the iachak, it is a way of cleansing impurities from the cells and imbalances from the mind. When we fasted in Ecuador, we still consumed liquids—typically chamomile tea with honey to hydrate the body and support the blood sugar.

Sacred Plant Medicine

As part of purification and healing, a person may drink medicinal teas that have been prepared by steeping one or more plants in hot water.

In my experience, I have found that I learn best what is resonant with my energy by working with a single plant at a time. If I make a tea of burdock, for example, when I drink it and then afterward sit quietly to see how I feel, I can more easily discern any effects from the burdock.

As Taita Alberto emphasized, it is not necessary to ingest a plant to receive healing from it. A person may sit quietly beside a plant and receive significant healing. This is another example of the workings of gentleness and intuition. Plants and all of Nature exude subtle energy. By analogy, we could say this principle is similar to a bird or animal who may hear sounds that a human is not able to hear. To say that those sounds do not exist is simple ignorance. To say that subtle energy does not exist simply because one has not learned how to perceive it is a tendency of modern, industrialized cultures, which have become very insensitive to the world about them. The person who wants to work with plants in a sacred way—in the way of medicine—needs to become humble and learn to listen. The practices of conversing with the elements as described below guide a person in entering sacred communion with the plant teachers.

As part of their iachak training, an apprentice may cultivate a garden, learning the unique properties and preferences of individual plants; this is a way of learning to listen to the plant—to see how it responds to certain conditions and to learn from the plant what is best for it.

THE AIR ELEMENT

The Air element is the life force. The life force enters the Earth element and animates it. When we are born, the first thing we do when the umbilical cord is cut is inhale—that is the beginning of our independent life on Earth. When we die, the last thing we do is exhale—that is the beginning of our journey free of Earth. When on Earth, we need our body and our breath. Many traditions of meditation and exercise emphasize the importance of the breath. For example, a meditator often centers their attention in the feeling of air entering and leaving the body.

In the Andean tradition, the Air element is associated with the mind and, therefore, is used to cure mental ailments. Taita Alberto spoke of the Air element as "lifting our heavy thoughts, our sadness, all the weights we carry in our lives, all the things we do not need in our lives." Practice with the Air element also brings into our lives what Taita Alberto called *transparencia*, a condition of being that is open and clear. "The Air [element] brings us health, intelligence, positive ideas, blessings, love, and prosperity," he said.[3]

Examples of ways of working with the Air element, in addition to the sacred communion described below, included Taita Alberto suggesting that if a person is having racing or negative thoughts, they can put a feather in their hair to help them release and cleanse their thoughts. Feathers are used in cleansings to move the Air element around and within a person. While doing a cleansing, Taita Alberto would often make small, clicking sounds as he wafted the feather, utilizing the Air element both in its moving capacity and in its characteristic of carrying sounds. He explained that the sounds help very small energies that are stuck in a person to release.

To the iachak, everything is energy, and energy always wants to move. When a person is caught in a negative thought pattern, this is a state in which the energy is stagnant or stuck, so the Air element is called upon to release the blockage. Taita Alberto often taught his apprentices to stand in the wind to release heavy thought patterns and emotions.

One time, during one of Taita Alberto's visits to me in Michigan, we were driving the back roads near my home. We were the only car on the rural, dirt road. The windows of the car were open, and we drove very slowly so we could see the fields, crops, and forests. There was a breeze blowing through the car. At one point, Taita Alberto asked me to stop the car. We sat in the car with the engine off while a soft, steady breeze flowed through the car windows, bringing the sounds of the fields and woods. We could hear the wind rustling the grasses and the birds conversing. As we sat there in silence, cabbage white butterflies floated up from the roadsides. Clouds moved slowly through the sky. Turkey buzzards circled over the fields. No other cars appeared. It was as if we had stepped outside of ordinary time.

Then Taita Alberto said, "When I have thoughts and emotions that I do not want, I allow them to pass through me, just like this," and he motioned to the window on his right and then very slowly and gently moved his cupped hand across his body as if scooping the air to release it through the window on his left. "I let these things move through me like this breeze moving through the car. It is not necessary to hold onto emotions or thoughts. It is good to let them move."

The practice of sitting meditation complements the teachings of the Andean mystical tradition. To know how to sit quietly, to see one's thoughts and emotions arising, to not attach to those thoughts or emotions, and to return to a quiet state is a fundamental, transformative practice that assists all those who are seeking inner development to recognize the strong hold of ego and to begin to loosen that hold.

In working with Taita Alberto, apprentices often experienced various emotional states. Some would attach to those emotional states, becoming angry or wanting a certain response from Taita Alberto or from other members of the community. For those already experienced in sitting meditation, it was easier to not allow those emotions to control their behavior and to instead allow whatever the strong thought process or emotional process might be to pass through the conscious awareness without speaking or acting upon it.

In the Andes, all insects and birds are considered to be carrying the energy of the Air element. When a feather drops in a person's path, it is a gift from Air and is received as such. An apprentice might pick up that feather and put it in their hair, or wear it on a beaded necklace, or place it in a shirt pocket over their heart.

To encounter the Air element intimately is to know what flying feels like. To fly is to be released from burdens that weigh down the psyche. To fly is to be within the reach of the Earth element, to see that world below, but to not be entangled in conditions that are always impermanent. To fly is to accept that impermanence as a gift. Flying is liberation. Taita Alberto said, "Let us fly higher and higher and higher. Let us fly in our dreams with the gifts the Air gives."[4]

Clothing and Color

To allow free flow of Air and elemental potency, the clothing of the iachak is chosen with care. The clothes are made of natural fibers—cotton, llama hair, or sheep's wool. The colors of the clothing are important too. It is said that white, which the iachaks often wear, radiates positive energy outward into the world and prevents harmful energy from entering the iachak's field. Darker colors, black especially, are said to attract more troubled forces. Taita Alberto would advise a person who was depressed to not wear any black. Kichwa women often wear black skirts, but underneath the skirt is a white cloth worn close to the body.

THE WATER ELEMENT

The Water element is associated with emotions and with the capacity to sense another person's state and also to merge with other beings. Water is fluid, boundary-less and, therefore, has the capacity to merge. Water is associated with the maternal and the ocean. Water also has the capacity to flow in spite of obstacles, finding its way through and around various blockages, so water is used in a curative way when a person is facing strong outer pressures that seem to be preventing them from moving in the direction their spirit feels called to go.

When experiencing purification in the Andes, we were offered various herbal baths and hot eucalyptus saunas as part of cleansing. At times, we would be given a bucket full of warm water that had been heated up over a fire as there were no hot-water heaters in the homes where we stayed. Various medicinal plants were gathered by the iachaks and placed in the water to steep. Then we would stand outdoors in the sunlight and pour the bucket of water slowly over head and shoulders and around the body to experience the soft, aromatic warmth and cleansing potency of the Water, Earth, and Fire elements combined.

At other times, we were taken to public saunas or hot springs where we sat in steaming, moist air where eucalyptus branches were spread on the floors and floated on the hot water. The pungent aroma of the eucalyptus cleansed sinuses and inner passageways. Following the sauna, we would take cold showers or submerge ourselves in icy rivers.

Also for purification, a person might bathe in water that has been steeped in various aromatic, astringent, and restorative plants. With the curative process of these baths, we see the mingling of all the elements: the Water element absorbs the medicine of the plants, the Earth element; Water is warmed by the Fire element; and the aromas emerging from the water float on the Air element.

Taita Alberto would often say that when a person moves into sacred communion with the Water element as described below, they not only cleanse their body, but they cleanse their internal organs as well.

THE FIRE ELEMENT

In Kichwa, the Fire element is referred to both as Taita Inti (Father Sun) and as Nina Mama (Mother Fire). Taita Alberto said, "The sacred Fire of life permits us to continue our lives. All the various forms of life are thanks to Taita Inti. The sacred Fire is within each of us. This is why the body has heat. The sacred Fire continually transforms and dynamizes life."[5]

The Fire element is associated with creativity and transformation. The energy of sexual union that creates a new being is associated with the Fire element as is friendship and warm-hearted encounters. If a person is lacking in vitality, it may be that renewing their conversation with the Fire element will be especially helpful. Taita Alberto spoke of the fire as dynamizing life. It burns negativities and infirmities, and it permits transformation.

To activate Fire, Taita Alberto would lead us in fire ceremonies. In Kichwa, according to Taita Alberto, there is no word for sacred. This is because everything is understood to be sacred. "There is no need to distinguish between what is sacred and what is not sacred," he would say. "That distinction simply does not exist in my culture." But to emphasize the sacred, to bring a person into conscious relation with the sacred dimension of being, ceremony is enacted.

In the fire ceremony, a fire is built carefully with attention paid to the shaping of the space where the fire will be and with reverence for the wood that will be burned. The shape of the circle is the feminine; the shape of the wood is the masculine. When the wood enters the circle, it is the sacred process of male and female uniting. A doorway is opened in the fire circle, facing south. It is through this doorway that the wood enters, and it is through this doorway that all offerings to Fire are given.

A common fire ceremony is the ceremony of releasing and of receiving. In this ceremony, the person puts into the fire everything they are ready to release. This is an energetic release. So, for example, a person may wish to let go of inner resentment. If so, they may walk for a time in the forest coming into conscious rapport with their intention to let these inner tensions and resentments go. When the person is ready, they select a branch, a leaf, or some other object they are drawn to, which will hold the energies they wish to release. Then they return to the fire, and while consciously speaking their intention in silence or aloud, they use their right hand to place the branch, leaf, or object into the fire. If others are participating in the ceremony, they may, at this time, be drumming, rattling shakers, ringing bells, chanting, or clapping. These rhythmic sounds help the energy release.

Next, if the person wishes to call in new energy, a new intention perhaps, they may then enter the forest again, now bringing into their awareness the new life that they are seeking. Again, when they are ready, they find a branch, leaf, or other object that calls to them, and they bring this back to the fire. With conscious intention, they place the branch, leaf, or object into the fire with their left hand, the heart hand, while calling in, silently or verbally, the new energy. Again, there is drumming and other song and movement as the person is calling in.

In the fire ceremony, the person does not hold onto expectations or demands, assuming, for example, that now all those resentments will have disappeared; nor do they expect that the new life will immediately make itself apparent. There is a gentleness and trust that is part of these ceremonies, giving over to what Taita Alberto calls "the Great Force of Life," the ultimate choice regarding what is best for the person. But the person now knows that they have done their part. They have consciously recognized what they need to change, and they have consciously chosen what they wish to have grow in their life. Remaining true to their path, they know that, in time, whatever genuinely needs to leave will leave and whatever genuinely needs to appear will appear.

Of the fire ceremony, Taita Alberto said, "Everything that you don't want in your mind, in your heart—put it into the fire. It will turn into light—beautiful colors—solar energy. The negativities are transformed into wisdom so we can continue our lives being lighter, carrying less weight. The warmth of Nina Mama illuminates us so we can walk the path of life with happiness."[6]

TEN

ENTERING SACRED COMMUNION

TO THE NEWCOMER, TAITA ALBERTO taught specific steps that help a person consciously and with clear intention engage in conversation with the natural world through entering sacred communion with Earth, Air, Water, and Fire.

Just as sitting meditation is a formal practice so, too, is sacred communion with Nature. As with sitting meditation, there is an actual structure, a pattern of transformation, that can be taught to those who wish to learn. To repeat, however, Taita Alberto emphasized that we should engage in these practices in a natural, spontaneous way. To follow training does not mean that the practices need to be forced or mechanical; it simply means that a pattern is being offered so the person who is new to this type of experience has some sense of how to begin.

The formal training begins with clarifying the person's attitude—their approach—to the natural world. For one who is yearning to activate their inner vitality and to live in harmony with the natural world, the practices that Taita Alberto taught will accomplish that—if the person is sincere.

Sincerity is more than desire; it is willingness to do the work. I have noticed over my decades of working with people that the single most important characteristic that determines whether or not a person will grow spiritually is that they are sincere, not ego driven, not needy, not tensely trying hard, but simply deeply sincere in their intention to learn and grow. That sincerity is the open heart, and the open heart is able to endure many trials and remain committed to the path.

That path begins with a recognition on the part of the human being that they are not above other beings, an acknowledgment that is humble and respectful and that is essential if one is to enter a true relation with the beings who share our world.

To reenter the universal conversation that all beings, other than human, are having all the time, the human being must first understand how to behave. Just as, in certain cultures, a child is taught specific manners for engaging in conversation with others, so, too, in conversing with the other beings with whom we share our world, there are formal conventions—ways to go about it that work, as opposed to ways that don't work. The person's attitude toward what they are doing— their thoughts, their gestures, their words, and their actions—may promote a genuine encounter or may interfere with and short-circuit the conversation.

Taita Alberto teaches students to enter into intimate relationships with the elements by consciously engaging in three simple practices. These three practices can be enacted every day, as part of ordinary life. The person does not have to set aside time, though they may at first in order to remember to do the practices. Gradually, these practices become part of the person's daily contact with Earth, Air, Water, and Fire as they move through their day. Taking a shower, preparing a meal, going to work, engaging with people—all the very ordinary acts of daily living are perfect opportunities for practice.

As a person is working with the elements, their thoughts and emotions begin to settle down and clarify. The intimate connection with the elements helps them process the fears and desires that create suffering. Sacred communion is a gradual process of coming to be more truly one's whole self. Because we are comprised of the elements, we feel our wholeness as we connect. When we feel Earth, Air, Water, and Fire, we feel ourselves, and we feel a condition of expansion, which is the Ushai growing.

We can see by analogy how this is so. A jaguar moving through the forest is not bound by ego fears or desires, worried about whether or not she is going to succeed. The jaguar is simply being her true self. So, too, an owl at night, a willow tree by the river, a cloud passing through the sky, the river itself—these beings already know their own way. It is only human beings who have lost their way. But when the human engages in sacred practice with Nature—when they lie down on the earth, wade in the river, stand in the sunlight, or inhale the fresh, morning air—they begin to feel, to sense, their jaguar-like original nature. This original nature arises through them. It is this feeling-state that relieves the person's fear and desire. In sacred communion, we are learning to simply *be* in direct, open awareness of all that we encounter.

When we enter conscious conversation with the elements, we begin to hear the sounds of the world, of *our* world. Taita Alberto referred to the Earth as *nuestra casa hermosa,* our beautiful house. In sacred communion, we begin a conversation with Mother Earth, with Ashpamama. Taita Alberto explained that in sacred communion, we "open the channel of communication" between ourselves and the elements. In using the word *channel,* Taita Alberto was emphasizing that there is an actual, energetic link—a pathway—between ourselves and others that opens when we do these practices. That channel has become dormant from disuse. The purification practices detailed above begin the cleansing of this pathway to make it possible to hear and to speak with other beings.

The process of opening this channel is similar to the process of making a telephone call. One person initiates the call, and when the other person picks up the receiver, the channel opens. Another analogy is that of electricity. When a person plugs a cord into an outlet, they activate the channel that will make it possible to turn their light on.

Or, similarly, to bring water into a sink, a person opens a spigot, and the water flows through the channel.

Through purifications, we cleanse the pathway, and when we then engage consciously in conversation with one of the elements, energy can flow in two directions—from us and to us. With the channels between ourselves and Earth, Air, Water, and Fire cleansed, we can again hear the teachings of all our relations. When we can hear the teachings, we can again participate in the way of rhythmic harmony.

To Greet

The first practice Taita Alberto teaches is *greeting* the element. This means consciously acknowledging the presence of the element. In silence or aloud, we say hello to Earth, to Air, to Water, to Fire. When we greet, we energetically make a formal bow of respect. This may be a literal, actual bow—a movement of the body that demonstrates reverence—or it may be an inner bow. Whatever the person is comfortable with is fine. The form is not as important as the energy—the sincerity with which the person greets.

The elements are always greeting us. If we are not paying attention, we are not aware of this. But Earth is always beneath our feet; the support the Earth gives us is a greeting. Air is always touching us; this touch is a greeting. Water is always flowing inside our bodies; this flow is a greeting. The Fire of the sun is always warming our world; this warmth is a greeting.

Taita Alberto taught us to begin a conversation with the elements by greeting them back! To greet the element is, first, an act of respect. It is an acknowledgment that the element is worthy of one's attention and is worthy of being recognized. This essential gesture of recognition opens the energetic channel between the element and ourselves.

We can do the practice of greeting in any time and in any place because Earth, Air, Water, and Fire are with us in every time and in every place. Not only are the elements outside our bodies, they are inside our bodies as well. If we feel separate from them, it is not because we actually are separate; it is simply because our attention is elsewhere.

A person's attention is a very powerful force. It is like a spotlight that illuminates and expands that which it shines upon. However, many people have little or no control over their own attention. It does not occur to them to "take hold" of the attention as the Buddhist teacher Thich Nhat Hanh puts it.[1] Instead, they allow their attention to be caught by external forces or internal emotions without any recognition that they can choose what energies they allow to flow through them by adjusting what they pay attention to. These ancient practices of meditation and Nature-based encounter train a person *first* to choose consciously what they wish to give their attention to and *second* to succeed in moving the attention in that direction. For example, a person may say they wish to pay attention to the sunrise, but instead, they may stand outdoors not genuinely seeing or encountering the sun because they are wrapped up in their inner process—thoughts and emotions. This is like going for a walk in the forest and looking at one's cell phone the entire time. The person's attention is not in the forest, so neither is the person, even though their body is there. Learning to direct one's own attention is the beginning of mastery.

When a person pauses before entering a forest and gazes at the trees, centering themselves and activating all of their senses, that person is directing their attention to the experience of encounter with another being—a life-form whose experience may be radically different from the human being. When the person consciously greets, they are acknowledging a level of equality between themselves and the forest life. The person who greets the forest has a different experience from the one who marches through the verge wrapped up in their own thoughts as if sleepwalking.

It is the act of greeting that opens the energetic channel between the human being and the other life-forms. If the person doesn't greet first, the channel does not open. As Taita Alberto says, "If we are walking in the city, and on the other side of the street, on the sidewalk, we see a friend walking, if we do not greet that friend, if we do not say hello, then the conversation doesn't happen. There is no encounter. The energetic channel remains closed." It is this open channel that allows the next step to happen.

To Feel

The second stage in the practice is to move into a quiet, open, non-judgmental state, a condition somewhat like listening—but without any attempt to "hear" something. It is a state similar to the spaciousness of sitting meditation. We do not push something away or pull something toward us. We do not *try* to have an experience after we greet. We do not set up expectations and wait for something to happen. Instead, we stand, sit, or lie down and quietly remain open. We activate our physical senses, putting attention into those channels. If we are greeting a tree, perhaps we touch the tree. If we are greeting Air, perhaps we pause and really feel the breeze touching our face. If we are greeting the sun, we stand and feel that warmth coming down to us. If we are greeting Water, we touch the water. Taita Alberto would often say, "Caress the water."

In conversation with the elements, we activate all of our senses. We listen to the sounds of the element. We smell the aromas that the element may offer. We see the form of the element or its movement or its effect on other forms that are visible. We may also taste the element, depending on which element it is or the effect that that element has on some other taste. We touch the element, as well, feeling its tactile quality communing with our body.

There is no push-pull, no attempt to manipulate or create an experience, no wishing, no fearing. There is *being*. It is in this quiet, open state that experiences arise that are not initiated or interpreted by the human ego and mind but that are, rather, a direct experience of human participation in Nature.

For example, a person is lying on a sandy beach on a warm summer day. They feel the warm sand beneath them and the hot sun shining down onto them from above. Their body is cooled in every moment by gentle breezes flowing across them, and they hear the sound of the waves lulling them in the way that a mantra or breath awareness may in sitting meditation. In this condition, any troubles or hopes that the person may have been thinking about prior to lying down simply evaporate. They are not present in the person's awareness at all. The mind, their Eagle nature, is quiet, but the person is not asleep. They are very awake. Instead of thoughts or emotions, the person is intensely aware of their physical experience. They are not "out of their body." They are fully in their body—even more so than usual because all the physical senses are engaged, and the person is aware of the sensory experience. In this state, the person feels extraordinarily peaceful. And then, time disappears.

This condition of vivid, awake timelessness might be described as floating or flying. It happens effortlessly. The person did not *try* to enter this state. They did not ingest psychoactive plants or utilize any techniques. They simply went to the beach for the afternoon, and Nature brought the person "on board" to Nature's perpetual experience of timelessness. This is the cosmos—this spacious, open flow. When mind does not interfere, we experience this state.

Reflecting on the experience afterward, the person may feel that their mind was temporarily washed clean. They may feel as if the breeze has just cleared the anxious thoughts out of their mind, or they may feel as if the heat of the sun has entered a sore, tight place in their body and released the pain. And though troubles and hopes have not disappeared from the person's life, they have experienced a genuine respite. They feel renewed and ready to take up their responsibilities again. Being in Nature in this way was once a common and naturally occurring experience. But in these times, many live fast-paced lives, rarely taking time to simply be quiet in this way. They may intend to, but life seems to take over, and they never get around to it.

This is why it is important to take up nature-based practice in the way one commits to sitting meditation. One needs to consciously choose to greet and feel each day. As the person gives themself more frequently to this state of timeless, awake presence, their sixth sense, the intuition, is given an opportunity to emerge. They become more available to receiving images, information, and insights that do not arise from their thinking process but that come from the heart, which is connected to the universal field of consciousness of which they are a part.

When I first heard Taita Alberto speak of feeling, I thought we were being encouraged to feel our emotions or to be aware of our emotions. But after listening more carefully, I realized that when referring to feeling, Taita Alberto was inviting us to put emotion aside in order to enter an expansive condition of full, sensory awareness, present-moment consciousness, and intuitive sensing of energy beyond the material.

Regarding emotion, Taita Alberto emphasized that emotions are the direct result of thoughts. In his view, emotions do not come from the heart; they come from the mind. Those thoughts might be so rapid, so automatic, and so unconscious that the person is unaware that the emotion they are feeling has been triggered by a thought process. For example, a tiger approaches; the person immediately feels fear without any awareness of an intermediary thought process. However, closer examination would reveal an assumption or thought behind the fear: tigers are dangerous. Another example: if a person contracted a severe skin rash, such as poison ivy, the one time they sat on the ground in the woods, that person may, unconsciously, hold a thought-form: sitting on the ground is dangerous and may feel an emotion of anxiety when asked to sit on the ground.

If a person experiences emotions during the feeling stage of the practice, this is fine. It is not unusual for a person to release long-held grief when they experience intimate contact with an element. In the presence of a beautiful, flowing river, for example, the person may feel so safe that they spontaneously release sorrow.

At other times, memories may arise during the feeling stage, and these memories may trigger emotions. This, too, is fine. Students often tell me that they remember how it felt to be a child playing outdoors, and they will say things like, "I haven't felt that way since I was ten," and they are smiling when they say it. They are feeling the emotion of happiness like they did when they were a child.

But the important point is that neither the emotion nor the memory is the goal of this stage of the practice. They are by-products. These emotional experiences are the result of having let go of any attempt to control or manipulate one's experience. The person is not trying to have an emotional experience. They are not trying to get in touch with a memory, but these things may happen as a spontaneous, natural occurrence that is part of their process at that time.

Different from emotion, the heart is the capacity to feel one's union with all of Life. Through intimate contact with an element, a person encounters the sacred dimension of being. This encounter develops and amplifies the intuition—the sixth sense. This is what Taita Alberto was referring to when he encouraged people to feel and open their hearts; he was encouraging them to connect to the energetic stream of mystical influence that is shared by all beings, by Earth herself and by the cosmos.

The development of the intuition, of the sixth sense, is part of the iachak training. A child reared in the Andes in a traditional way, as Taita Alberto was, may have this intuitive capacity—the Condor heart—fully active. But a child reared in the North, as I was, may have been trained away from this capacity by hyperrational emphasis separating the "real" from the "unreal." So, a child from the North, for example, may be told that dreams are not real; while a child from a traditional family in Ecuador may be told that she is traveling at night and visiting other realms that are equally real to the daytime world and that offer information and guidance.

As the heart opens more, a person feels less generalized fear—fear with no actual cause. With less fear clouding their awareness, they can sense when they are on target or off target. There isn't as much need to be "right"; there is simply interest in learning and in growing.

In the feeling stage, the person experiences an encounter with the sacred dimension of being. This encounter is profoundly healing, and it is not the result of any teaching or wisdom a human teacher could impart to this person. It is the result of the person allowing the stream of energy that is their original nature to flow.

To Express Gratitude

Sometimes this encounter with the sacred spontaneously generates a song or chant. While walking in the woods, a person may simply begin singing. In their open, expanded feeling-state, a song arises. The song or chant is an expression of the peace that the person is now feeling. Sometimes they sing in their own language; other times, they are simply making sounds or singing in words that they do not recognize. My own experience of this process includes a feeling of lightness and spaciousness.

The spontaneous expression that sometimes emerges as song was described by Taita Alberto as a natural expression of gratitude. There is a feeling of happiness and joyfulness that is beyond what we typically call emotion. It is a feeling of energy flowing outward from the person, as if they are a small sun and their inner forces are streaming outward into the world. The song is the streaming forth of the person's feeling of wholeness and completeness. It is the way they naturally join themself to the process that Nature is doing, and the song—the joy—is itself an energy force that completes the healing.

It is not surprising, in this context, that traditional healers usually sing and chant while they are conducting healing ceremonies. Many sources describe individual medicine people or Indigenous practices that include song and chant as a guiding feature in the healing process.[2]

Traditional shamans say that the world is made up of sound. This is not meant as a metaphor. It is meant literally. Joan Halifax describes the Dineh perception:

> The Dineh understand that all beings, be they star or stone, are condensations of sound, solidified vibration. To connect with the medicine, or power, of lightning or star, one must sound them. Medicine singers of the Dineh use chants as keys to open the mysteries of seemingly uncontrollable and unpredictable nature.[3]

To the shaman, sound is a wave that travels through the material world. It is a vibration that becomes matter and that can rearrange matter. Just as an opera singer hitting a certain note can shatter a glass on the other side of the room, so, too, for the shaman, sound can be used in healing to rearrange physical substance.[4] In the Andes, a iachak musician who is conducting a healing ceremony will sometimes use a flute made from the bone of a bird or animal that corresponds to the place in the human body that is perceived to be holding the illness.

For those who are cut off from the feeling-state, it is important to cultivate a formal practice of expressing gratitude. When they express thanks each time they drink water or each time they eat a meal, they maintain the energetic channel between themselves and the elements that they opened when they greeted. To maintain that open channel throughout one's day is the path of the iachak. In so doing, they increase the life they can receive. Their receptive channels begin to open even more.

Taita Alberto emphasized that the joyfulness a person feels during the feeling stage of the practice is, itself, a form of gratitude. Our happiness is an energetic gift that we are giving back to the elements themselves. To illustrate this principle of natural, organic, effortless reciprocity, Taita Alberto gave this example: "When a mother has worked to prepare food for her child and has prepared the food with great love and care and then gives the food to the child, and when the child loves the food and eats the food with great pleasure, then the mother feels great happiness."

This natural, reciprocal energetic loop is what maintains the lives of human beings and all their relations. Taita Alberto always emphasized that when we express gratitude to the elements, we receive more gifts. And he would remind us that whatever we need in life will arrive, for us, in a natural way as a result of our sacred communion. "We must visit, again and again, the mountain, the waterfall, and these gifts will arise in our hearts. We will receive what each one of us needs in this moment. It will come in a natural form. We will be able to flow in the different circumstances of our lives. We will receive exactly what we most need."[5]

On the journey to Ecuador, Taita Alberto began by connecting us to the Earth element when he invited us to lie down on the ground. Throughout the subsequent days of the journey, at the subtle direction of Taita Alberto, we experienced various encounters that highlighted one element more than the others. Soaking in hot springs, bathing in water with aromatic herbs, and drinking herbal teas helped cleanse our internal organs and connected us with the Water element. Our many walks and sitting at a high altitude in meditation led us to feel the power of the Air element. Sitting by the fire at night, listening to stories and being reminded of sacred traditions, illuminated our minds and opened our hearts to the Fire element. All these were spiritual exercises of cleansing and healing that help the mind and the heart regain equilibrium—that encouraged the Condor and the Eagle within us to fly again in the same sky.

RETURNING TO EARTH

Taita Alberto's invitations and teachings were aimed at assisting people who had become divorced from Nature to return to the innate rapport with the Earth, the sacred communion that their ancestors knew. He often said that these practices had been saved by the ancestors for these times.

Initially these three steps—*greeting, feeling,* and *expressing gratitude*—may sound too simple to be powerful. People from industrial cultures sometimes come to shamans of root people seeking a big experience. They anticipate something dramatic and intense, something that happens *to* them, that will somehow shake loose the blockage that they feel. The simplicity of Taita Alberto's teachings—to greet, to feel, and to express gratitude—causes some students to not realize their potency. "Surely," some ask, "there must be more to it than that? Surely, I need a power plant or some complex, secret technique, some arduous test in order to arrive at this longed-for state?" It certainly was the case that sometimes those who worked with Taita Alberto did experience something dramatic that shook them powerfully like an earthquake. But just as the traveler seeking a shaman in South America may be guided away from the women iachaks who hold such deep power, so, too, a person who is looking for something "big" may never receive the healing they seek. If they remain embedded in their industrialized-culture belief that power is a dominating energy, they may miss the true teaching. If they do not realize that true power is a quiet, internal state, they will not travel far.

The seeker must understand that the key to their own healing is to become willing to quietly practice daily in a way that is subtle and largely invisible, like the Mama Iachaks—a way that requires letting go of the projects of ego. If the person sincerely wishes to enter sacred communion, they will experience great healing through feeling and greeting Earth, Water, Air, and Fire and expressing gratitude.

These practices are the agents of change. Through these practices, we reactivate our innate capacity to converse with the beings who share our world and, thereby, to understand our place in the large currents and great forces that move life.

As many have observed, the characteristic method of the shaman is to bridge worlds. This act of bridging worlds is medicine. The shaman travels from one level of reality and perception to another. To cross over from one level to another is the path of healing. As Joan Halifax puts it: "The shaman has the duty to help restore balance by opening and renewing the lines of communication between realms."[6] It is specifically these lines of communication that Taita Alberto sought to teach his students to recognize and to cleanse.

The practices of greeting, feeling, and expressing gratitude open the *heart*—a corridor of energy. These practices initiate the seeker into the world of the Condor. A person can attend many workshops and diligently study Indigenous ways of being—theorizing, taking notes—but never truly *experience* their Condor nature because they remain in the Eagle side of their being. They haven't greeted, they haven't slowed down to feel, and they haven't expressed gratitude, so they remain embedded in their wounded state—the state in which the Condor and the Eagle within them are not yet having a conversation. For truly, we must remember, each of us contains both of these powers at all times. Taita Alberto always emphasized that he was not saying that *heart* is better than *mind*. Both powers are needed to fly harmoniously.

When Taita Alberto was working with young people from his Indigenous community, he emphasized the powers of the mind, of intellect and reason, of planning and taking steps to realize goals. Depending on who he was working with, Taita Alberto taught how to activate whichever power was suppressed and how to join the two together so the person could fly, so they could live from their whole human being.

The training of the iachak includes developing the capacity of discernment. Characteristic of the condition of genuinely receiving information and insight is that while it is happening, the person is not experiencing any emotion. Later, upon reflection, they may feel emotion in response to what they have experienced, but initially, in the open condition of feeling, the person simply receives.

When a person activates the *heart*—their *intuitive knowing*—they begin to transform at a cellular level. The body begins to relax. The relaxation of long-held tension in the body makes possible a shift in the person's mental formations. Their emotions settle down. Their thoughts become healing thoughts. They no longer waste time with negative thoughts, and they know how to gently dissipate such thoughts when they arise. Their vision clears. They see a broad perspective as if they are flying high in the air. Without emotional attachment, they perceive below them multiple possibilities and are able to choose the path that most contributes to the well-being of all. Their actions now come from clear thoughts, their thoughts come from using their intellect and reason without the confusion of emotional interference, and they sense intuitively what is most in alignment with Nature, with the healthy continuation of all life. Thus, they do less harm, and because they are doing less harm to themself and others, they feel happier. Even when they are suffering because of illness, losses in their personal lives, or dangers and imbalances in the world, even when they are very aware of these things and are experiencing them, they still have a reservoir of clear seeing and deep peace that they can tap into within themself. And it is this that gives them serenity in spite of the trials that are part of human growth.

They also experience more patience, more patience with themself and more patience with others. They realize that they are always walking the path, that it is not about arriving at some ideal, perfect state but about a process of encounter—encounter with other beings and with themself and with the realization and sometimes the actual experience that those others *are* themself. Yes; there will be times when they will encounter difficulty, will lose their way, will forget to practice, will feel confused, but there is no judgment in this. This is simply part of being human and walking in this life—a life that is for learning, not for acquiring. So when they stumble, they simply recognize that they have stumbled, and with no waste of energy in self-blame, they step forward and continue.

This is the path of the iachak, this is the path of the runa—to continue. Often, Taita Alberto would say to us, *"Adelante!"* Forward! Always forward.

PART THREE

THE CONDOR
VISITS THE
EAGLE

ELEVEN

FOR THE YOUNG PEOPLE

THE FOLLOWING IS MY TRANSCRIPTION of a talk Taita Alberto gave to my students at the University of Michigan, Ann Arbor, in September of 2003. He spoke in Spanish with a translator. Any errors in understanding are mine.

•••

I come from the Andes of Ecuador. My culture is a root culture. It is pre-Inca. We have a conception of life that is different from modern life. This difference is valuable because it allows us to share with other cultures. As part of our cosmovision, we see life as a great circle. We don't see life as linear, beginning at one point and then going forward.

This concept of time allows us to integrate everything we do in life.

Something simple that we may do in our daily lives may have an important effect. For example, to visit a waterfall is very important to us. The waterfall is not only a physical phenomenon—a liquid. When we are with a waterfall, we are being with Life—with a distinct type of life. The waterfall is a being that communicates with us, and we can communicate back with it. Of course, it is natural that a waterfall does not communicate in the same way we do.

For example, we communicate with Water by singing. This song we do from the heart to communicate what we are feeling.

We have observed that people who come from the city and who try to communicate with Water: they are thinking about communicating whereas we are feeling.

For us it is very important to feel the communication, not only to think about it. We can use a song. We can use a chant. Or we can use a different way of expressing what we feel.

This action of thinking is a characteristic of the Eagle. It is a power of the Eagle. This action of feeling is a characteristic of the Condor. It is a power of the Condor. The Condor is the largest bird in the Andes.

It is good to think. It is good to feel. It is good to feel and to think.

When we express how we feel to the Water element, this produces a special reaction in the water, and it also produces a special reaction in us. For example, people who communicate this way feel peace and tranquility inside. And as the water is flowing, it begins to express more sounds. This is the way the water and we are communicating.

We benefit mutually. The water benefits, and we benefit. The same is true of Earth, Air, and Fire.

When we have a problem that is very great, for example, we may go to the mountain to help us with this concern. We go to communicate with the earth, with the rocks, so that we can discover what it is that is creating our disquietude.

I do not have words that are adequate for describing the type of communication that happens. It is a state that is related to feeling. But we believe it is something very important in our lives because it helps us in many ways.

Like everyone, we have things we want to learn about, things we want to know. To learn, we go to the elements, as I just explained with Water. We can do the same with the Wind, Earth, and Fire—with whatever exists in Nature. I hope this explanation is somewhat clear. Would you like to ask me questions?

QUESTIONS FROM THE STUDENTS

Q: How do you know when you've made contact with Nature and the elements?

You don't know with your head. You feel it. You feel fulfilled. You have met Water. It is natural for the mind to say "What? You didn't hear anything!" It is possible the mind will say "You have not yet established communication because you haven't heard anything." But this type of communication gives one a special feeling of tranquility and later, possibly, when you return to the house or the next day, a solution to the problem comes.

Q: How long have you been like this? Did you come to this at a certain age?

I don't know what my age was, but my first memory of this is being with my father and feeling this way. I remember that he took me to the mountain. He took me in his arms, singing and carrying me to a natural spring. He would sing to the water, saying, "Let us play with the children in the water." After a while, in reality, I was there in the water with many children. And then I was in a state of not really sleeping but somewhat like sleeping, and I was still in the arms of my father. I had a very beautiful sensation of having played with the children that were in the water. As I grew up, it wasn't as much playing with Water as it was learning what Water had to say about life.

Q: How does this connection affect your life, how you see your life and your work?

I hadn't noticed that it had a special impact on my life. I thought this way was natural with everyone. But when I met people from the city, I realized this wasn't so for everyone. They did not feel Water. They did not feel Earth. They thought Water and Earth had no life. So they could not imagine that they could communicate. That's when I realized it had been a great gift to receive this education. So now my experience is that this is an essential part of what I do in life.

Q: Can you feel the same communication when you are in the cities?

Yes, but it takes more effort.

Q: What is your work?

I don't have a job. I have never worked. I never thought about working. I think people should do what they *like* to do. If they are doing what they like to do, then it is not work; it is play. Yes, I have had jobs in the past, but they were play, and if they did not remain play, then I did not continue to do them.

Q: What is a typical day like for you?

I try to wake up when the sun rises. The sun, the day—have their own life. I begin to establish communication with the day, exactly as I did when I greeted you. I greet the day. I greet the sun. I greet the place where the sun rises, and then also the other directions, and then the interior of the Earth, and I end with the upper cosmos.

Then I bathe. I have breakfast. It isn't the same every day. Each day has its own activity. Sometimes I have to climb a mountain or help with things in the house. Sometimes I cultivate in the field—if it is the time for that. I help with milking cows. There are many things that one does on different days. Sometimes I think that after breakfast, I have to go into the forest. But maybe a person shows up who needs my assistance. Normally, we have lunch around noon. We have conversation about the things we have done, what we still have to do, and we decide what each one of us can or should do.

We may be doing things until five in the evening. Then we return and make dinner. We discuss what happened in the day, what results we had. We have dinner, and we talk some more. The younger ones may have more trouble going to sleep, but generally we go to sleep around nine. That's because now we have electricity. Before, when the sun set, we would go to sleep.

Many times I just escape and go to the river and do the things I already explained. Because of the responsibility that I carry within my communities, I do different things—like healings. I travel a lot—to Bolivia, Peru, Colombia, Central America, the United States.

It is not very exact, very routine in my life. It is not possible in my life to say what I am going to do a month from now.

Q: How do you maintain hope and conviction given how the world is now?

I think it is my responsibility to contribute so we put a stop to those negative things that we are doing. I have to maintain harmony so I can project more harmony. The conflicts that are in the world are created because of imbalance. The least I can do is try to acquire harmony and balance so these can project outward.

As I said in the beginning, any small action that we do has repercussions. I don't think that in order to solve a problem we need to create another problem. I need to do as much as possible to project harmony—for example, if I respect the life of animals. One form of respect for animals is not eating them. Animals project much harmony.

Q: I am interested in the practice of chanting. How does this relate to feeling?

[*Taita Alberto drums gently and chants softly in Kichwa.*] If in a while you asked me to repeat this, I could not. This is what came out in this moment. This is a form of connection. In this case, I sang to Water. I felt Water. I felt the water that is in my body, and I said what I felt at this moment. I think the chant should be natural.

The form of teaching that I use is not the same way that you are doing in this classroom. Those who apprentice to me, they do so by doing things with me, various activities on a given day. They follow me, and we do the things we have to do that day, and they converse with me. For example, when we have visitors from abroad, I have to have some of my students there helping me.

We can only share these things by doing. Of course we talk, after each meal, but not during the meal because that is a special time for communicating with the Earth. It is the love of the Mother Earth coming in through our mouths. It is not possible to feel this love while talking.

We have a school for formal education. But when we leave there, we try to maintain part of our culture. It pleases me very much to share with the young people because they are the ones who will carry on this knowledge that we have.

Now, according to our prophecies, young people have been born who have very ancient knowledge. This time—this *pacha*—is for old people from the past times to come in bodies of the young to show the wisdom they have inside, and for this, the only thing they have to do is to feel.

They feel more and more each time. It is very easy when it is done in a natural way. But it is very difficult when one *thinks,* when one asks: "How am I going to accomplish this?" This activity of feeling the wisdom one is born with is not a function of the mind; it is a product of another ability we have, which is the ability to *feel.* I am not talking about emotions—emotions come from the mind. I am talking about *feeling* [intuition]. All people have this ability. All people have the Condor within them. All they have to do is train, practice more daily habits to unblock the channels for feeling.

Q: What kind of daily activities can we do to help us feel?

Greet everything that appears before your eyes. You do not have to do it aloud if you fear people will think you are crazy [*laughter*], but we can do it from within, from deep within. Greet the sky, the trees, the water—greet everything you receive. Remember that in order for two people to communicate with each other, they first have to greet each other.

Another thing that helps a lot is to not eat animals. Another thing that helps is exercise. Another that helps much is to look at the horizon when the sun is rising. Another thing that helps is to listen to water as it is flowing, to listen to the sound of the leaves as they are moved by the wind. Another thing that helps is to watch the stars.

In these actions, we are not looking for anything specific. We are simply allowing the connection to be established. There are other simple things, but with this we can start.

Q: What does the word *shaman* mean?

The word *shaman* is not in our language. It was created by a writer, possibly an anthropologist. The responsibility that I have in my language is called *iachak*. My responsibility is to maintain our traditions, to establish communication with the different manifestations of life, to share with others so they will have the capacity to feel. This is to help others so they can act in a natural way in any circumstance.

For example, if there is no car, then the person can walk. There is no need to make it an issue. In a natural way, the person can find solutions; they can create and refine.

We do not need to look in the head for a solution because a solution is closer than one might think.

The person can feel relaxed when in a difficult situation. They do not necessarily need to think for the solution to come. They can feel their own harmony. In the harmony the solution is found.

If a person is in harmony when running, for example, the person does not need to become tired. To react in a natural way when there are situations that may affect us, to not have an internal reaction—to be upset by something that is unplanned—this is a sign of our harmony.

Q: Can you give an example of the type of healing you do?

To help people open their channels, for example, I use the elements of nature—plants, flowers—I sing or chant to Mother Nature asking for her to help the person. With the feather of a Condor, I move around the body, singing to Air. With Fire, a small piece of wood that is burning, and I pass it close to the body. We spray water close to the body.

In Kichwa, our language, we have five elements, the fifth element is called Ushai. This element is the product of the union of the four elements. In order for the Ushai to help harmonize the person, we ask the Great Force of Life to enter the person and protect the person, and we follow this shape through the body.

Then we give thanks to the Great Force of Life for this opportunity to cleanse the person, and I express that both myself, the healer, and the person who is healed are part of the Great Force of Life.

In our community, we might go to the waterfall or to the mountains, or to the forest. It is not something showy or dramatic.

Q: In your tradition, what is your view of death?

To me, death does not exist. It is impossible for anybody to die. Only the body stops functioning. We are not bones, flesh, and blood. We are that something that makes this body function. We are not the body. This something that we are is part of the Great Force of Life. It is part of all life. The body has a beginning and an end, like all the plants, all the animals—but no person dies. What changes is the external appearance.

For example, when a child leaves his body, then in my community, we make music. We dance. I know that in the cities it is different. People cry. They suffer because they think everything ended. But the person who left the body—if you want to communicate with them—go to bed, go to sleep, and you can converse.

Perhaps there are people here who have had communication with people who have died in their dreams. It isn't something that is hard to believe. It is real. So let us greet the dreams when we are sleeping so that when our body is sleeping a lot of dreams will come.

The person who leaves the body continues living in another body. There are many realities. This is only one. Some believe that this reality is the only reality. That is not true. There are many realities that exist, and many solutions and many discoveries exist in those other realities.

One form of communication is to travel to another reality. It is possible to do this every night when we go to bed. Our bodies remain resting while we travel to other realities. It is natural. Everybody does it. It is a cosmic law, like the law of gravity.

Any time a person sleeps, they leave their body. Many people forget because when they awaken, they may move rapidly. Then they forget their dreams. Or maybe they had a lot to eat at dinner.

Q: If you had a chance to meet the leaders of the United States, what would you like to say to them?

I would tell them they would be better leaders if they could feel more because people are going to follow more strongly if they feel more. In history books, some leaders in the past have used this technique I am talking about. Current leaders, we need to invite them to feel, not only to think. But it is not necessary to fight them to make them change. They are soon going to leave their bodies.

You are the ones who are going to be the leaders. It is you who will eventually fill these spaces. The great majority of young people don't like this form of leadership. Therefore, the young ones someday will do differently when they are in that position. It is just a matter of waiting for the right time and space.

And we all need to make an effort to feel more. It is possible that for some of us here, the winds of life will take us to very high positions.

Q: Do you believe that there will be an end of time?

Time is not linear. It is circular. Only something that is linear has a beginning and an end. Time in this reality is a little rapid; it is cycles like spirals. In other realities, time is different. For example, when you sleep in this reality, you may sleep for an hour, but it is possible that what you experience in a dream may cover a lot of time. When you awaken, you may say "I only slept a short time."

In another reality, time is not necessarily as it is here. To illustrate this, visualize two spirals that intertwine. One goes very slowly; the other can be experienced very quickly. Time is intimately connected with space. In Kichwa, we don't have a different word for time and space. It is one word—*pacha*—because it is impossible to separate both things. This is the moment during which we are talking; this is the place in which we are talking. Can anyone separate the two? Only the mind in the Western world does this separation.

That's why time is very different for each one of us and even more so in other realities. This conception of time is very important for us. For example, if someone is singing, in order to feel what she is singing, she can't at the same time be thinking "I need to go to another class." In that moment of time, she is feeling that connection and cannot be thinking about something else.

Time that is measured does not allow us to flow in a natural way. When you want to experience *feeling*, you need to forget about everything else and enter that time-space of feeling where time disappears. You enter in whatever way you want. Some may enter by singing; some by dancing—every person has a special way to enter that space of feeling more.

Q: Do you believe in a supreme being or that Nature is God?

Nature is the supreme. Nature is everything. Everything is a part of the cosmos, and each one of us, including these chairs we are sitting on—in my conception—is God. God is not a person looking down from above. God is very, very big. It is the Great Force of Life that is in each of the things that exist in the universe. It is everything.*

If we wish to be specific, if we narrow down and try to define God, then it becomes nothing.

Q: Why do you visit other countries? To teach and learn?

I visit them because I have invitations, and I honor them. I travel to Peru, Bolivia, and Colombia to meet with the elders.

Traveling to the United States began as a fulfillment of a prophecy. This prophecy says that someday the Eagle and the Condor will fly together.

The prophecy said that someday the people from the Andes would come here to share and that people from the North would come to share in the Andes. It is important that people with the Eagle way acquire the way of the Condor, and it is also important for us to acquire certain aspects of the Eagle way of life.

I come to share so we can create more harmony. However, if instead of sharing we try to impose one culture on another, then we create disharmony. Every culture in this world is very important; this gives us the very beautiful opportunity to share from the heart and with respect.

The transcriptions of chapters 12, 13, and 14 were taken in handwritten notes at my home in Duirhaven, Michigan. Taita Alberto spoke in Spanish. These notes are my translation in the present moment of his words. These transcriptions capture the way he spoke, which was very simple and beautiful at the same time. Any errors in understanding are mine.

---

*For further discussion of Taita Alberto's conception of God, see chapter 14.

TWELVE

LEARNING TO WALK TOGETHER

◆

Duirhaven, September 2003

Friday Evening

We are beginning to walk together. We are having a conversation. I don't want you to think I am going to teach you. We are going to learn together. We are going to open the heart a little more—every time a little more.

The teaching does not come from me. It comes from the Great Force of Life. The teaching will come from the hearts of each of you. Each of you has wisdom within. That wisdom that is within you is what we are going to draw out.

Ask yourself this question: "Why am I here?"

Feel your answer.

We sit quietly for a few minutes.

We sit quietly with our eyes closed for a period of time.

◇◇◇

It is natural that when we begin to walk together we start to know each other. As we progress in knowing each other, it is easier to walk together. It is healthy that we can share along this path our dreams—and different, individual dreams can come together to be one, great dream.

On this path, a great dream can be transformed into a simple but grand dream that helps our life, that heals our heart, that cleanses our mind, that fills us with joy, with the beautiful feeling of life.

With that nourishment, we can then help others. Helping ourselves along the way, we are also helping others. As we open our hearts each time a little more, we also help others to open their hearts a little bit more.

This question: "Why am I here?" What helps us discover the answer? This question is going to help us on this path. It will not be answered completely, now. This is a process as we walk together.

After these brief comments, Taita Alberto invited everyone to go outside and notice a tree, plant, or shrub that called their attention, to go to the plant and greet it, and then sit quietly with the plant until we heard him drumming. Upon hearing the drum, we returned indoors and shared a small meal together. Then participants returned to their homes and arrived again the next day for the afternoon gathering.

Saturday

When we greet each other, a channel of communication opens. We greet the day. We greet the six directions: north, south, east, west, the sky above and Earth below—everything. So we are then connected with life itself—always, in every place and in every moment.

If I don't greet a person, that channel of communication does not open. This channel opens easily when the greeting is from the heart. It is the same with the elements. We must greet them if we wish to open a channel of communication with them. I know spiritual people who work with the elements but forget to give gratitude. When we greet the elements, we give gratitude also. Not giving thanks is like wanting to go into the room where there is wisdom but not being willing to open the door.

This learning is not restricted to this reality. The world of the dream is another reality where we can learn. Even if we don't recall dreaming, it doesn't mean we haven't dreamed. It's just not recorded in our physical body, and even if we don't recall our dreams, they still have an effect on us.

In the path that we follow, each one of us will encounter something very simple that will help us. We will find that which we need. The Great Force of Life knows exactly what each person needs. The Great Force of Life exists in each one of us; we only have to open the channel of communication. Therefore, it is necessary to clarify in our minds that we are not going to find—in this learning—something extraordinary but rather something small and simple. Something that everyone needs. These small and simple things will help connect us to the Great Spirit of Life and to knowledge of the path that each of us should follow.

We each need to follow our own path.

In general, the mind looks for something very special, something very big. It is for this reason that the mind says, "You need to study more, to learn more, to read more."

But you already have walked a long way. Now is the time for each of us to determine that which is needed in our path. The experience of learning with me does not include a lot of information for the mind. My intention is that each of you will learn more, that each of you will open more the power of feeling—every time, more and more, opening different channels of sensitivity. This will complement the information you already know.

I am aware that sometimes the mind will be in conflict about this. But remember that this is the time for the power of the mind and the power of the heart to fly together. We have to have the clear idea that this is the time when the Eagle and the Condor fly together. The Eagle is the characteristic of the people of the North, the mind. The Condor is the way of living in the Andes, living from the heart.

Up until 1989, the focus was on thinking. For humanity, thinking was very important. The time before 1989 was the *pacha*—the Kichwa word for time and space—for thinking. These years now, since that time, are the pacha for feeling. Therefore, we are in the stage that we don't use *only* the mind, and we begin now to feel more and more. We don't fight the mind, but we also don't follow *only* the mind. We fly with both the heart and the mind in harmony.

This is the responsibility of the Andes now—to invite more the path of feeling. It is not about a new religion or new techniques. It is the invitation to take advantage of what we already know in order to feel more, to complete our life, to fill our life with more sense of purpose.

In this process of learning, it is necessary for you to visit and to know the Andes. Let us remember that words are limited. By visiting the Andes, walking through the mountains, and visiting sacred places, you have an opportunity to learn without words.

What I am speaking of should not be taken as a belief, or a philosophy, or a theory. It is a reality.

Taita Alberto stands up and invites everyone to come outside with him. Together, we call in the six directions—facing north first, turning clockwise to the east, then to the south, then to the west, then to the Earth below us and the sky above us. We do this in silence. Then we sit down outside with him.

◆◆◆

In the six directions, we encounter different forms of expression of the Great Spirit of Life. A special force of the Great Spirit of Life is found in each of the directions. Remember there are not only four directions, there are six: north, east, south, west, the Earth below, and the cosmos above. When we salute the six directions, we open the channels of communication. We need to greet the six directions and the elements in Nature. When we greet, it is important that we greet with our heart.

In the beginning, all these channels were open. Babies have their channels open. The society and the way of living either close them off or open these channels. The habits of our lives help open or close these channels. Therefore, beginning with saluting the directions and the elements continually will help us clean and open these channels.

It's an action from our whole heart—from our feeling. If we do these practices but don't feel while doing them, they become mechanical, as if we are pushing a button to receive a result. These practices have immense power if we are feeling. It is the same practice, but if we do it mechanically, it will not serve us and will not have the same results. It is for this reason that we cultivate spontaneity and creativity.

Being spontaneous and creative are ways of the heart. Techniques and trying to be "accurate" are related to the mind.

It is important to remember that we are not, in any moment, fighting against the mind. Both are essential: the mind and the heart, thinking and feeling, feeling and thinking. The Eagle and the Condor, flying in harmony daily inside us.

What I invite you to do is to begin with certain habits in your life because it is not enough to *know*: to know is very important—to know things—but what is essential is to *live* what we know.

But the mind will say, "No, I need to know more." We have to remember that habits can close and cut off our communication—can close our channels. Now is the time to dynamize, to incorporate other habits, habits of our daily life—simple things that we can do in any moment and in any place. Every time we do this, we can receive a gift. We must open a channel of intimate friendship with everything that is a manifestation of life—everything.

We can begin with ourselves. Have we greeted ourselves this morning? Our body is marvelous. We are not this body. In general, the mind thinks that we are this body, but we are not this body. We are not the bones, the flesh, the blood. We are that something that gives life to this body. So we need to greet our body because it is an immense gift from the Great Spirit of Life, a gift that makes it possible for us to live in this reality.

That is why we need to feel our body, and we need to be aware of how we treat our body. How are our rivers? We talk about cleaning up the rivers on this planet, but do we take care of the rivers in our bodies?

Habits are very important to our path. It is important to practice what we already know. There are many things that we know—many techniques, many philosophies. Now we must select and practice— whatever techniques you wish.

In the same way that we can start by greeting our body, we can start by greeting the elements. The elements are close to us. We use them all the time. Yesterday, we gave thanks for the gifts that we receive. This is another habit that helps us to clean and open our channels.

We can take advantage of the moment in which we breathe to give thanks to Air, and we can repeat this every moment if we wish. Each respiration is something to give thanks for because it is sustaining our life.

In the same way when we eat, it is the love of the Earth coming to us. Everything we eat is the love from Mother Earth coming to us. We must feel the love of the Mother that is transformed into the Earth through colors, aromas, tastes, textures. Mother Earth did this for us, her children. She did this with love for many months. We are her children—her sons and daughters—and we need to be grateful to her for what she gives us.

Many people say that they want to feel a connection with Mother Earth, or they say, "I love the Mother Earth," but when they eat, they don't feel the love for Mother Nature. They don't feel the love, and they just throw away what is left over without respect. Changing this habit will help us cleanse our channels of connection with the Mother.

We must take only the quantity of food that we can use. How can we connect with our Mother if we throw away her gift? It is not enough to say a prayer before our meal and then to waste the food. There is an abundance of food on our table, and we should be very grateful. Because you were born in circumstances where food is abundant, you must use it wisely and appropriately.

Possibly in the same moment that you have abundant food, in another place there is no food.

It is necessary, sometimes, to practice fasting. This helps us cleanse our bodies and value our food. Perhaps you fast one day a week. In other places on this great home, our Earth, there are people fasting because they have no food. They feel immense gratitude for very little food.

Because I feel that it is the love from Mother Earth, I have an intimate connection with Mother Earth. I receive infinite gifts from the Mother, and the least I can do is not waste it. Another form is clothes. The first time that I came to this world of the Eagle, I saw people wasting things that could be very useful in the Andes.

Abundance is a blessing, but it can transform into its opposite when it is not used correctly. But also poverty is a blessing because it helps us feel immense gratitude when we receive a simple thing. You can see small children running barefoot in the fields with happiness glowing in their eyes. So every person is born in the circumstances that they needed. We need to be grateful for these circumstances and use them well.

Material poverty can also be a danger. Those who don't have material things think that when they do have them they will be happy. But material things are not essential. Yes, they complement life, but they do not create life. We see that those who have a lot are bored. They want something more.

What *is* essential is to feel gratitude for what we have and to use it in the best way we can.

Money is not good or bad. It depends on how each person uses it. Money can help us walk our path in harmony. If we don't use it well, the same money can be a hazard—not only for us but for others.

I hope with this example that it is clear that we should feel grateful for what we have and that we should take advantage of the circumstances each of us has. It is very, very important that we be grateful for our circumstances—whatever they are.

This is an introduction to a form of learning that we have begun to acquire and that we will continue to acquire as we walk this path together.

Every time you breathe, you can greet Air. You can feel the air entering your body and bringing you life. Every time you exhale, you can express gratitude. When we achieve this connection with Air, respect and gratitude are born in a natural way. It is not necessary to think, "Oh! I should give thanks." We just do it naturally. We don't have to *think* it is something grand because that greatness is *felt*. We *feel* the importance materially and spiritually of this element. We become aware that we depend on this Air element and on the other elements. We are part of that Great Life, and that Great Life is part of us. To know the physical characteristics of Air, to feel the power of Air—both are essential.

The same is true of Water. It is not only a chemical formula; it isn't only an odor or color—Air has power, Water has power, and their characteristics are very grand. To know this with the mind is different from experiencing it with feeling. When we do both, the Eagle and the Condor are flying together.

It is the mind that makes assumptions and assumes limitations. For example, the mind might say that if you live in the country, it's going to be easier to connect with the elements. But the reality is that Air and all the elements are in all the parts of ourselves and of Earth. If we feel this intimate connection, then we are going to be able to experience the elements anywhere, anytime.

All the elements that are outside are inside us as well. Inside us are rivers and forests and deserts. Because of this, we must be ecologists of what is inside us as well as of what is outside us. I know many people who fight to protect Nature and the elements outside themselves but their own rivers and Earth inside them are contaminated.

This path that we have taken is to live fully in every moment in every place—to experience all of our senses all of our life. Not only to experience the pretty things but to experience everything fully.

Let us consider Fire. Fire constantly dynamizes life. We have the fire ignited inside our bodies. One of the external manifestations of this fire within us is the warmth in our bodies. Another manifestation of the sacred Fire is the love that we feel and that many times we cannot convert into words. Many root cultures speak of the sacred Fire. Many times the mind says, "In order to create the sacred Fire, we need a large space so we can build a bonfire." This is an external form of Fire, but each one of us has the sacred Fire lit within us. This sacred Fire illuminates our lives. This sacred Fire makes colors come alive; this sacred Fire makes us see in a very simple thing something sacred.

In my Kichwa language, the word *sex* does not exist. In order to use this word in Kichwa, we say "the sacred Fire." Because of the sacred Fire, we all have bodies. Through the sacred Fire, our mother and our father gave us our body. The sacred Fire allows life to continue.

But if someone uses the sacred Fire without respect, it can burn a lot. Many people reject the sacred Fire, considering that the sacred Fire is not sacred, thinking that it is very material, very much of the body. The sacred Fire is very powerful. The sacred Fire permits us to transform from one state to another. With the sacred Fire, we can illuminate life, or we can have the same fate as a moth when it flies into a flame.

Let us remember that we are not insects. We need to be illuminated by Fire but not burned by it. We need to be able to feel the warmth of Fire but not to get burned. We need to keep the sacred Fire alive, but not let it take over. The sacred Fire is not used to end or terminate things but to constantly illuminate. The sacred Fire is meant to transform us constantly.

The time that we are living in now is also the time of woman. And women are the ones who can best utilize the sacred Fire. I have seen that the Statue of Liberty is a woman with a torch—now is the time of women to illuminate the path with the sacred Fire. Cosmically now there is clarity that this is the time of the feminine aspect. And if you observe in these days the activities of the world, you will see that more feminization is happening.

In Kichwa, the names of the elements of Nature are feminine:

> Nina is Fire
> Yaku is Water
> Waira is Air
> Ashpamama is Earth.

Ashpamama is Mother Earth where we live. Pachamama is the Great Cosmic Mother, Mother of Time-Space. On the path, a time-space can be difficult and then later it becomes easier and then it becomes difficult again and then it becomes easier. This helps us because we can learn a lot when it becomes more difficult. We feel that this difficulty helps us. And then it becomes easy again.

Sunday Morning

We first went outside and greeted the earth, the water, the air, and the sun. When we returned, Taita Alberto drummed and chanted to each element in Kichwa. Then Taita Alberto asked people to share their experiences after leaving the workshop the previous evening. Some people shared dreams they had experienced during the night.

◇◇◇

If you wish to remember your dreams in the morning when you wake up, do not move. The head and spine need to be in the same position until you have remembered what happened during the night. Open the eyes, breathe a little, and then you can close your eyes, until the memory starts coming back.

The Great Force of Life determines which experiences you remember and which you don't. Whatever you need to remember, you will remember.

All people who are part of this path can communicate with each other in the world of dreams. When we have a commitment to this path, we continue at night in this relationship. There are a lot of experiences in that reality that we don't have the capacity to comprehend. So The Great Force of Life keeps the mind quiet, and we may not consciously remember. But all manner of experiences that happen register and are recorded. When it is time, we will remember them.

Also it is a suggestion to help you remember your dreams to have something by the bed that you can reach without moving your head so you can write what has happened.

Remember that habits are important to incorporate into our lives. You don't need to have someone check up on you and ask if you did this or not. You can do these practices in your homes. Let us remember that the path I am inviting you to is not more theories or more philosophy; it is to practice what you already know. We have already walked a long way; this path is to implement, to put into practice, what we know.

The recommendation is that just before going to sleep, you give thanks for the day, for all that has been learned, and that you give thanks for this opportunity to sleep and visit other worlds.

For me there is the day of the sun, and when I am sleeping, it is the day of the moon. I recommend that you give thanks to the day that has concluded and also greet the day of the moon that is beginning. The form that we use, the way or the time that you choose, is up to you. What is important is the spontaneity and creativity of each person. What is essential is not to do it in a mechanical way or by obligation. We do it as we feel it from within our hearts—feeling what we are doing.

So what we are doing is emphasizing that we do these practices from our hearts so we can connect through our channels with the Great Force of Life, so we can cleanse those channels of communication. Those channels have been blocked because of habits that have blocked them.

We need a culture that is filled with habits that help us clean and open those channels—a culture that leads, step-by-step, toward harmony. It is different from the current culture. Our actions and activities must be filled with the heart so we can transcend the current culture.

When we do these simple things, they will open doors for us. When we feel more, we are drawn to what we dream of reaching, we are drawn to where we want to be—to that thing that we are looking for. Certain of our characteristics have locked or closed these doors; other characteristics are going to clean and open these doors. Let us create habits and abilities that help us harmonize our lives.

When a person is greeting naturally, they approach the element in a friendly manner. The plants, the stones, the animals all possess the same great value that we have ourselves. We are life with a certain appearance. The plants, the stones, and the animals are life with a different appearance. Yes—even the stones are life. This is a reality because everything that exists in the world contains part of the Great Force of Life.

Therefore, when we greet a plant or a tree, it is not the external appearance that we are greeting. We are greeting that which is within the physical appearance. When I greet a person, it isn't the physical person that I greet. I greet that which gives life to that person's physical form. The physical appearance is very important because we go through the physical in order to greet the life inside.

Now, with this clarity, we are going to walk through the yard and in the woods and touch, with respect and gratitude, something from the vegetable world.

We walk greeting, feeling, and expressing gratitude. When we return indoors, Taita Alberto guides us in another practice.

◈◈◈

Now we are going to again touch a plant or tree while we sit here with our eyes closed. I am not inviting you to imagine. To imagine is different from actually leaving our body and going outside and touching a plant. In our mind, the difference between doing and imagining is very small. It is easier if we do not think while we are doing this practice. We need to feel. Practice will allow us to distinguish the difference between imagining and what is real.

Let us not be surprised if while doing this we come across our physical body sitting or lying down. This is a small introduction to traveling without the body. These are the places where we learn without words—feeling that we are part of what we are learning.

To feel, for example, that we are part of the chamomile will help us to know what the purpose or use of the chamomile is because we *are* the chamomile.

We sit quietly with our eyes closed for a period of time.

◇◆◇

We only did this for a few minutes. It requires more than an hour and practicing at various times. When we were children, we did this naturally. At night, every night, we do this naturally. The difference is that we don't think that we are going to travel; we do not plan and decide or try. We just go to sleep and do it.

In order for the body to rest, it is necessary for us to go out of it.

When we do things with feeling, our consciousness grows. These things are not from the imagination. They are from our consciousness. In order for us to expand our consciousness, it is necessary for us to feel.

When we are feeling life in every moment, we will start to have more clarity. This is the way of living with wisdom. This will help us to realize that everything is sacred. In Kichwa, there is no word for sacred because everything is sacred. We feel from the smallest to the largest that everything is sacred.

My intention is not to teach things that give you weight. You already have this. For example, it is not necessary to feel bad about wasting food. We don't need to take on any more burdens. We simply change our habits. As we change these habits, this helps us lighten. We begin to feel released. My intention with these practices is to start to lighten the load, so we can fly—weightlessly.

Many people in their lives are traveling with a lot of baggage that is totally unnecessary. But the mind thinks we should carry that load. In this path, we are going to climb mountains, so we need to get rid of our baggage.

Remember that everything we face is an opportunity to walk our path. When we eat, an opportunity to increase our intimacy with Mother Earth is given to us. Every time we breathe, an opportunity for an intimate relationship with Air is given us. When we feel the warmth in our bodies, when we feel friendship and love, this is a channel of communication with the sacred Fire. To drink water, to wash ourselves, is a great opportunity to clean the physical part as well as those other aspects that need to be cleaned. In this way, our life becomes transparent and fluid.

Every element, everything, exists in this reality to help us let go of what we need to let go of and to receive those gifts that we need to receive. For this reason, every moment and every circumstance is an opportunity.

In one culture, one thing is good, and in another culture, that same thing is bad. For one person, rain is a good thing; for another, it is not. This depends on what you think is good or bad. In my way of thinking, I do not have a conception of a separation between good and bad. What exists are simply circumstances. For example, a person may say, "I do not want this to happen." He prays that this does not happen. This thing happens, and he suffers. Time passes. Then he realizes how he has changed and what he has learned and gives thanks for what has happened to him.

The Great Force of Life knows exactly what we need and exactly how to give it to us. It is better to say, "I think *this* is good for me, but you, Great Force of Life, know better what is good for me." It is important that we decide what we want, that we head in that direction, that we do what is possible with our hands to create what we want. But if this is not meant to happen, we will start encountering obstacles. It is not about doing nothing and waiting for something to happen. It is to flow, not to be stuck in a place. Accepting does not mean giving up or conforming. It means flowing with it.

But the great majority of human beings, they don't do this.

Remember that *I* am not your teacher. The true teacher is waiting within us. Our practices, our habits are our teachers.

When our actions are directed to harmony, when we, bit by bit, are loving children of the Mother, we are fulfilled. The great majority of humanity are ungrateful children of the loving Mother Nature. Some may express or say that they love Mother Nature, but with their actions, they show a different story. We need to be consistent with what we say and what we do. In a simple and sincere way, we need to apply the things we already know—a reflection, with sincerity, of everything that we have learned. Then our minds will be more tranquil.

It is our mind that says I need to know more, learn more. The invitation of my heart is that we act and live according to our dreams—to what we wish for. I'm not saying that knowing more is a bad thing; it is just that knowing more is a greater responsibility. It is worse if you do a thing when you know you are not to do it.

These are simple practices that help us feel more—simple reflections that help us understand the greatness that is in simple things.

When we went to touch a plant or a tree, we received a different form. I have seen people tear apart a branch, thinking they are greeting a plant. But we must greet the plant in the same way that we greet a person whom we love.

The sacred Fire is another very subtle food that helps us nurture our spiritual body and path. We give thanks in the moment, and we practice feeling with our heart inside the intimate connection.

When we are going to practice in our lives these things we have spoken of, they will become more fluid and more natural. It is natural that at the beginning we ask, "Am I doing this right?" Let's remember that these activities that we do on a daily basis will help us feel more. We will cleanse our channels. This brings harmony.

THIRTEEN

RIGHT TIMING

◆

Duirhaven, March 2004

THE PATH OF EACH ONE OF US IS FILLED with surprises that many times the mind classifies according to cultural notions, according to educational and social precepts. These surprises are classified as good or bad, while in reality, we cannot label circumstances as good or bad at the moment that they happen. After time passes, we can see with more clarity.

There are many things that we do not like at the time that they happen. But in the future, we may realize that it is best that it happened this way. This you have confirmed in your own lives many times. This is a great truth of life. But when we have experiences that we don't like, we forget about this truth. We only want things that are to our liking. We do not thank life for the difficult circumstances.

Humanity has reached the height of a very complicated way of living. We forget very simple truths. I hope you have reached the limit of this complex living and accept the great truth that circumstances cannot be classified. It is natural that all of us want circumstances that we like. If we are having a pleasant experience, it is easy to live in plenitude. But when it is not pleasant, then it becomes difficult. But life has then given us a grand opportunity to set in practice what we know: meditation, the breath, food, and many more things that we know. The more difficult the experience, the better. It gives us the possibility to discover ourselves.

We can ask, "How am I? Who am I?"

If we look for the answer with the mind, then it is very difficult. How do we open the door to the answer? We apply what life has taught us. No one learns what they do not need to apply.

But at a certain point in time, a person will need what they have heard or read. In that moment, we have the opportunity to apply it. The answer arrives. We take the next step. And when we take the next step, we realize that this was meant to be.

Another obstacle is impatience. We want an immediate solution. The world is a grand, living organism. We are also living organisms. The world has its heart. We have our hearts. Both hearts pulse simultaneously. If we don't apply patience, our heart beats faster and disharmony begins within us, and that has an impact on the world. Millions of impatient people are altering the rhythm of their home—this Earth.

We can ask, "What do we want to be?" Step by step we discover what we need to discover. Nobody discovers before or after the right timing. Everything has its pacha; its time-space. This is exact.

I was in northwest Colombia in the Sierra Madre Mountains learning from the Kogi. I was in a very special forest. There were many mosquitoes, snakes, and animals and many sounds—like a whole symphony. I was learning with a *mama.** And I asked this guide, "What do I do with the things that I've learned in life?"

I was sent to a small mountain in the middle of the jungle. I was told that once you go there and you find the answer, then you can return. I spent about ten days tormented by mosquitoes. It was very useful for me because the experiences one has outside are a complement

---

*The Kogi name for the elders who teach.

to what one has inside. So many days fighting internally—against the mosquitoes, against the noise. I was trying to find the answer according to what I wanted—no noise, no mosquitoes.

And there was a lot of heat. Then the answer that I found was that what was happening outside was similar to what was happening inside—inquietude.

This is our tendency to evaluate, to classify, to separate everything into good, bad, better, best. Life should not have to be what our mind wants it to be. Life has to be the way we internally need it to be. No circumstance is without a purpose that can help us awaken.

A few days ago, there was a rebellion by the Indigenous people in Ecuador. Four people were killed but possibly many more. I was in the mountains, so I did not participate directly. But the army was looking for me in the last city I was in before I went to the mountains. They thought I was directly participating, but I was in the mountains. I didn't know what was happening or when it would end. Many people told me it was dangerous for me. But when I got to the city, everything had ended.

The mind can tell us many things that are not real and can take us to despair or fear, and outside circumstances can look bad to us.

Around 1990, many guerillas were active in Peru. I was invited to speak at a conference at the University in Lima—to speak of what I do. I took with me a book that had a red cover. On the cover was my photo and the title of the book: *Iachak and the Indigenous Uprising*. At the conference, I sold many books, and the ones I still had I took to the next city where they had invited me to speak.

In the middle of the route to the city, the army stopped the bus, and they detained me with the book. They covered my face with a hood. They tied my hands and put me in a car. They drove for a very long time. After a time, we arrived in a place very hidden. They put me in a very dark room.

I could hear how others were being beaten and shot close by me.

My mind said, "This is my end." I felt a lot of fear. I don't know how much time passed, but to me it seemed like a lot of time, and then I heard steps. They untied my hands and took off my hood so my mind said, "This is the end."

I said to the Great Force of Life, Jatun Pachakamak, "Thank you for this great life you have given me and now receive me." But nothing happened. They took me to an officer, and they asked me if I had been helping the guerrillas. I replied, "I fight so there is more harmony, so that this conflict will go away. This book advocates a peaceful revolution."

I don't know my books this well, but a page number came to mind. I said, "Look at this page. It says my philosophy," and I told him a page number. The officer opened the book to the page I had indicated. There he read, "It is not necessary to use a single bullet. It is necessary to transform ourselves." My mind did not know that this was the correct page.

The officer asked, "How can I change myself?"

I saw that he had a problem with his liver, and I told him to drink a lot of water and to take herbs. "That is what I do," I told him. "So follow my advice."

He asked me how I knew that he had this problem. "Do you have information about my life? Maybe it is dangerous what you know about me," he said.

I told him, "I do not know about your life. I only felt that you have this problem." The officer didn't believe what I said about the herbs. I told him I would go to the market and buy these herbs, so he sent me to buy them. I went to the market. My mind said, "Now I should not return." I spoke with a woman about these herbs and asked, if she gave me the herbs, could I come back with the money. She said yes. I took the herbs and went back to the officer.

He saw the plants and said, "Yes, others have recommended these."

And I said, "This is what I do. This is my work. I do not look for change through violence." He gave me back my books and money for the herbs, and he set me free.

It is natural to react with nervousness or fear, sadness, crying, and suffering when our life is not going as we wish. But we are now learning to walk not only with our mind but also with our heart. This is how we transform our suffering.

Life is going to give us the answer, and the door is going to open. When? When it is the right time. The mind says, "I want it fast." To want is not bad, but we need to understand that it will happen at the right time.

When we are always searching for the connection with the Great Heart of Earth, the natural way, the natural form, will arrive, and the doors will open.

It is not in a logical way. That is mental. For example, the logical mind says, "This is one sound; that is another." Logic is important for things that are purely material. The power of the mind is really important in those realms. Material things have a beginning and an end. Then there is the antimatter, which sustains the material. We also call this the spiritual or intuitive part. Yes, we need the mind, but we need to allow, each of us, more space for the intuitive part to participate.

Equilibrium is a word that each of us may have a different conception of. For one person, an executive in a modern company, what we are doing right now may seem out of balance. That person may think of this market economy where every minute counts. But to us, we who are following this path, that crazy race of the free market seems to be unbalanced. So how do we know?

We know because we *feel*. Equilibrium is to feel that one is in balance with oneself and with everything else that exists—applying all of what we know.

Regarding our economy, now is the time when the market should be at the service of humanity, not humanity at the service of the market.

Whatever we are doing, we can find ways to be in more equilibrium and to experience more joy in what we do. When we listen to everything our mind is telling us, we start receiving all kinds of emotions, including sensations of anxiety. So when my mind is confused, I take advantage of that experience to express to the Great Force of Life, "Here you have me. You decide what to do with me. I am ready to do whatever you require of me to do."

Each time it is not an expression of the mind, it becomes an expression of the heart—without fighting to find the answers, without wanting the answer, and without saying it should be fast or slow. Maybe the answer arrives in an unexpected way. Maybe it is what one least wanted, but this is how we learn.

What I am *really* is "that something that takes action" in these moments of despair. The body cries that it feels hunger, that it feels despair. What we learn is, in reality, we are "that something that comes into connection with the Great Reality." This is Pachamama, the Great Cosmic Mother. Ashpamama is Mother Earth. Pachamama is the Great Cosmic Mother.

Ashpamama, this Earth, is physical, chemical, material, and can be divided into the very small. The body is part of this Ashpamama. But there exists something that sustains the material part—this is the spiritual part, and everything in the universe has both.

Materially, we are composed of the same physical aspects, but in the energetic field, each one of us has more or less of the spiritual part. The degree of spiritual quality differentiates each physical person. The degree of spirituality affects their way of being.

We always can grow spiritually. I suggest that we open our path. As we walk, we are opening our path. To do this, we are creating our destiny as we walk. So we need to have patience as we walk, accepting the truth that impatience brings suffering, and patience brings peace and joy.

If we accept and feel this truth, then we feel peace because we know the answer will come. The answer will come through the action that the person takes. But do not confuse patience with inactivity. The mind measures time as long or short, but time is not exactly as it appears. For a person who is suffering, one minute is equal to eternity. For a person who is in joy, years could seem very brief. Therefore, it is better to not think of time as something linear—long or short, fast or slow. So we are patient, and we take advantage of circumstances no matter how difficult. We have the ability to learn from them by opening the channel of communication.

Each one of us will communicate with whatever we feel close to—whatever is part of our belief system. Most likely the answer will not come to the mind, and possibly it won't be immediate. But if we keep the communication channel open, it will come in its own way and in its own time.

FOURTEEN
RECEIVING GIFTS

❖

Duirhaven, May 2004

Healing Ourselves

If we become paralyzed by noticing the harm others are doing, we do not do what we need to do. It is important to know the importance of Nature; more important is to act in harmony and to *feel* Nature.

You know perhaps many people who want to help others to be more sensitive, but you may have seen these people unable to act in harmony. They are activists. They preach and defend, but when they eat, they don't feel the love from Mother Nature. For example, they waste food or they contaminate their own internal rivers.

Let us consider Water. We think Water is very different from us. But when we connect with Water from our heart, then we feel and we understand that Water feels, Water listens, Water speaks. We feel that this is true. These are not beliefs. It is something we know because we have felt this truth.

Water reacts according to how we treat her. Water outside us reacts to how we are feeling. If we think and feel love for Water, Water will react and feel the same way for us. For me, one form for helping with

151

the contamination of Water is for us to think and feel that Water is clean and not contaminated.

Then Water, at the molecular level, begins to rejuvenate herself. But if we think and feel that Water is contaminated and dirty, we contaminate Water more.

To help a person, we should not think of them as sick. We should think and feel that person is getting better and better.

The body of a person will respond to how others around them think and feel. The Water element is part of this dynamic. Because we have so much water in us, we are responding to and taking in the water of others.

Everything Is Food

When eating, it is necessary to feel much joy. To enjoy is a form of giving thanks for the gifts from the elements. In food, all of the elements are united—Fire, Water, Earth and Air—and the harmony of these elements produces the fifth element, the Ushai.

When we are connected with these gifts, they have a very special energy. Therefore, we are going to eat this energy that fills our heart and spirit. We should never eat just to fill our stomach. We need to eat to fill our heart, the spirit, and also the stomach.

When we are at the table, we need to be conscious of it—to be conscious that this is not only for the stomach, and it is not only for our eyes. It is also what we smell. Each element that is on the table has a lot of energy inside—the energy of love, light, and wisdom. Therefore, everything we eat is a great opportunity to penetrate the secrets of Nature. Because food is Fire, Air, Earth, Water, and Ushai, everything in the food, on the table, in the kitchen, is God. We are going to eat God. God will be inside us. God is life and creates life. This is the food. Food has life, and it gives life.

In reality, food is everything and everywhere. It is inside and outside. The food is Air. The food is sunlight. The food is different aromas.

Seeing each other is food. Touching is food; listening is food; speaking, singing, dancing are food. Everything in life is food.

The mind thinks of food as being for the stomach only. It is only one type of food that is for the stomach. There are many foods that we receive through the eyes. This gorgeous, brilliant green is a special food. [*Taita Alberto touches a rosemary plant beside him and turns to a woman near him who had asked for help with her child's behavior difficulties.*] If your son sees more green, he will be more tranquil.

According to the conception of food that we have in my culture, this is how we are nourished. If we ingest laughter, then we are feeding the heart. Every activity that comes spontaneously from our heart is a very special meal.

Therefore, are we in agreement that everything is food? Food for the stomach, for the heart, for the mind, for the emotion, for the body, for the spirit, for the eyes, for the ears—everything is food! And all of us are fed. Everything feeds everything else. Our senses are food—to see is a special food, to touch is a special food. The sacred Fire is a special food. When we realize that everything is food, we receive a very special gift.

Everything Is God

Ushai is the word we use in Kichwa to refer to the union that comes from the combination of the four elements. We experience the Ushai when we have the awareness that we are not separate from the elements. That moment is very hard to explain. In that moment, you *feel* that you are Water, Fire, Air, Earth—it is the Great Manifestation of Life. It is the Great Spirit of Life. There is no difference. It is necessary for us to arrive there.

A little obstacle is the mind. When you greet, when you make this connection, you do not need to think of it in words. You do not need to decide what words you are going to say. It's not important that your mind understands. It is like a person who doesn't know how to cultivate plants. If someone asks them to explain, they do not have the experience. But after the person experiences the whole process of plant-ing, harvesting, and eating—then they begin to *feel* what this means.

It is very good that we have been able to share these things. None of you are lacking the tools. All of you have the tools that each one of you needs. Therefore, for the next time that we meet, I invite you to share anything you would like about your experience with this intimate contact.

Intimate contact with Nature is an important step to contact with the Great Force of Life. If we salute and greet with respect intimately with the elements, it will be easy to give a greeting and respect to God. Everything that exists is part of the Great Spirit of Life. Each one of us is a part of the Great Whole or All.

Depending on cultures, times, epoch—they have given different names to this. In Kichwa, Jatun Pachakamak is a name we use.

When spring arrives, what do you feel? You don't have to think in order to feel this. You just enjoy. This intimate contact with the ele-ments, with God, is the same, and the person is filled and remains fulfilled. The person could be naked, could do things that others call crazy. In Sanskrit that is the special state called samadhi. This is the time to experience samadhi. To live in samadhi.

I have given you, in these two days, the keys. Through these keys, you can open the door. We feel and unite intimately with Mother Nature. The words are not important. What is important is the con-nection with the Great Spirit of Life.

That Great Spirit that gives us life in Water and other elements of Nature. If we flow together with the elements of Nature that are tangi-ble, that we can see, that we can have inside us, if we flow with Nature without thinking, not worrying, we are going to flow in the wisdom of God.

Inside our conception, God is not up high, not far away. God is in all parts in all moments. Therefore, we have an opportunity to be with the Great Spirit of Life everywhere and every time—to be in a permanent connection with the Great Spirit of the Universe, with the truth that is beyond mind.

It is not true, as history says, that we are worshipping the sun, the moon, the mountains—what they saw was an action of connection with the sun, the moon, and the mountains, an action of respect and gratitude toward these elements of Nature.

This time that we are living now is for living in a spiritual way. This time is not for thinking "Am I or am I not spiritual?" This time is for affirming that we *are* spiritual, for *feeling* permanent spirituality in everything. This is the time for experiencing that *everything* is spiritual. Every action—all action and reaction—has to be *felt* in this way.

In some philosophies, they speak of this ecstasy, this samadhi; it is the feeling of plenitude. This feeling you can learn to prolong more and more—this samadhi—*sumak alli kausai!*—the full life, the complete life. This is to be with God, to be part of God, to not think that God is far away and one is abandoned. Don't think this. This is not true. We need to feel the truth. God is with one, and one is with God. It is necessary to *feel* God in every place and in every moment and in every activity. We do our activity feeling this—to eat, to sleep—feeling this is the great power of Life.

So we cannot be unconscious and eat without expression. If we are conscious that food is God, then a natural expression comes out that food is God. You agree that God is and gives life? You agree that food has life and gives life? Therefore, it is all one thing.

We should not forget this. The spiritual path, the path that we are following, is not theoretical. This path is totally practical from moment to moment in every time and in every place. We are in agreement?

OCTOBER 23, 2005

More of Taita Alberto's teachings on the divine came in an encuentro *(encounter) in Niles, Michigan, at the home of Mikkal Smith, a North*

American shaman and director of Crows Nest Center for Shamanic Studies.

◆◆◆

God—Jatun Wyracocha Pachakamak Pachakuti—is very big and also very small. It is everything. Also it is nothing. There is not one mind that has the capacity to understand the greatness and the simplicity of these words.

Mother Earth, Ashpamama, is within the Great Mother Nature, Pachamama. Every element of Nature is within the Earth, and the Earth is within the Great Mother. The Great Mother is the tangible expression of the Great Spirit of Life. And all of this—the elements, Earth, Nature—is one thing, the Great Spirit of Life.

And we also are a part—an essential part. We are not far away from God. We are not under God. We are a part of God, and God is a part of us. Pachamama is the fountain, the source, the spring of the material life, and also is the spring of the spiritual life. We are all an essential part of the expression of life. You are essential. The cat is essential. Nothing is more or less. It simply *is*.

I am. Every one of you is. We should feel this truth. I am. I am part of an immense thing. I am big, big, big. But also I am nothing. *Soy nada.* It is not about others seeing me as big or small. It is about them seeing that I am. I am part of that little, little thing as well.

So why worry? Preoccupation, worry is in the mind. When we understand these things, we feel gratitude. It emerges in a natural way. And you feel love toward yourself. Much love toward what you see. Much love toward what you cannot see. When we are experiencing this feeling of gratitude and love, this is happiness.

Happiness is not an objective we are heading toward. Happiness is a continual, permanent expression from ourselves—and also from the outside.

EPILOGUE

ON THE JOURNEY FROM NORTH TO SOUTH, we carry maps that portray the outer terrain, delineating mountains, tracing rivers. But where is the map to the inner journey? Where is the guide to that wandering, never arrow-straight Way, the interior road that leads to the jeweled inner life?

In cultures of first peoples, it is the shaman—the person who carries medicine—who guides this inner journey. It is the shaman who maps the inner terrain with chants, with flutes made of bone, with rattles made of seed, with drums made of agave and goat skin. The shaman sounds these vibrations to unite the one who journeys with the cries of birds, the rustle of trees and grasses in the wind, the soft fall of rain, and the heartbeat of the Earth. Birds, plant life, rain, and the ground become allies of the human beings who, without these supports, would lose their way, caught while sleeping by coyote trickery.

When the shaman chant, the bone flute, the seed rattle, and the hollow drum cease, we discover wings that have mended. We soar above the ground, freed of the belief that we can do nothing to save our world.

GLOSSARY
OF KICHWA TERMS

Allpamama: Mother Earth

Ashpamama: Mother Earth

Atau Allpa: The Great Incan Being who keeps the worlds in balance

Chacra: The family garden

Hanak Pacha: The Higher World

Inti Raimi: Celebration of the sun and summer solstice

Jatun Pachakamak: The sublime creator of time and space

Jatun Taita Iachak: The Highest, Father Iachak

Kai Pacha: The Middle World, the tangible world

Mama za: Mother dear

Nina: Fire

Nushukpacha: The New Era

Pacha: Time-space

Pachacuti: One-thousand-year epoch, divided into two five-hundred-year periods

Pachamama: Great Cosmic Mother

Pushkana: Spindle

Runa: A person who is committed to spiritual growth

Ruray: Taking action in a sacred way

Shunguan: Love from the heart

Sumak: The ideal, the highest and most beautiful

Sumak alli kausai: The highest expression of lifestyle in harmony with Nature

Taita: Father

Ukupacha: The Lower World/The coming era of dissolution

Ushai: An all-pervading spiritual force

Waira: Air, wind

Waranga kutin shamushun: By the thousands we return

Wyracocha: Creator

Yaku: Water

Yupaichani: Thank you

NOTES

INTRODUCTION. BECOMING A IACHAK'S APPRENTICE

1. Taita Alberto, email message to author, April 4, 2017.
2. Tatzo and Rodriguez, *La Vision Cosmica de los Andes*, 14.
3. Taito Alberto, "Levantamiento Indigena del Inti Raymi 1990 parte 2," posted by spott179, YouTube video, 9:59, May 28–June 8, 1990, speech at 5:31.
4. Perkins, *The World Is As You Dream It*.
5. Berry, "An Agricultural Journey in Peru," 3–46.

CHAPTER I. IACHAK MEDICINE: THE BIRD PEOPLE

1. Halifax, *The Fruitful Darkness*, 19–20.
2. Reichel-Domatoff, *The Sacred Mountain of Columbia's Kogi Indians*, 31.
3. Tatzo and Rodriguez, *La vision cosmica de los Andes*, 33.

CHAPTER 3. THE LOVING EARTH

1. Boyd, *Rolling Thunder*, 87.

CHAPTER 7. TIMELESSNESS

1. See for example Silko, *Ceremony;* and Perkins, *The World Is As You Dream It*.

CHAPTER 8. THE PATH OF THE RUNA

1. Recording of Taita Alberto by Helen Slomovits.
2. Recording of Taita Alberto by Helen Slomovits.
3. Berry, *The Dream of the Earth*, 41.
4. Halifax, *The Fruitful Darkness*, 81.
5. Recording of Taita Alberto by Helen Slomovits.
6. Mindell, *Dreambody;* and *The Shaman's Body.*
7. Taxo, *Friendship with the Elements*, 99.
8. Rumi, *Selected Poems*, 155.
9. Amergin, "The Mystery," trans. Douglas Hyde, Midwest Institute: Ireland Study Trip (website).
10. Wordsworth, "Ode: Intimations of Immortality from Recollections of Early Childhood," 228.
11. Taita Alberto, email message to author, February 21, 2007.
12. Toelken, "Seeing with a Native Eye," 17.
13. See, for example, Ereira, *The Elder Brother Speaks.*

CHAPTER 9. PURIFICATION AND THE FOUR ELEMENTS

1. Taxo, *Friendship with the Elements.*
2. Blake, *The Marriage of Heaven and Hell.*
3. Recording of Taita Alberto.
4. Recording of Taita Alberto.
5. Recording of Taita Alberto.
6. Recording of Taita Alberto.

CHAPTER 10. ENTERING SACRED COMMUNION

1. Hanh, *The Miracle of Mindfulness.*
2. Halifax, *The Fruitful Darkness*, 81–91; and Buhner, *Sacred Plant Medicine*, 42–48.
3. Halifax, 82.
4. See Massachusetts Institute of Technology, "Breaking Glass with Sound," YouTube video, 1:15, 2010.
5. Recording of Taita Alberto.
6. Halifax, *The Fruitful Darkness*, 193.

BIBLIOGRAPHY

Soon after I began working with him, Taita Alberto changed the spelling of his name to Al ver to, with spaces between each syllable. Publications in Ecuador from the 1990s spell his name Tatzo or Taczo.

Berry, Thomas. *The Dream of the Earth.* San Francisco: Sierra Club Books, 1988.

Berry, Wendell. "An Agricultural Journey in Peru." In *The Gift of Good Land.* San Francisco: North Point Press, 1981.

Blake, William. *The Marriage of Heaven and Hell.* New York : Dover, 2012.

Blancke, Shirley. *The Way of Abundance and Joy: The Shamanic Teachings of don Alberto Taxo.* Rochester, Vt.: Destiny Books, 2022.

Boyd, Doug. *Rolling Thunder.* New York: Dell, Delta, 1974.

Buhner, Stephen. *Sacred Plant Medicine: Explorations in the Practice of Indigenous Plant Medicine.* Boulder, Colo.: Roberts Reinhart, 1996.

Caddy, Eileen. *Opening Doors Within.* Forres, Scotland: Findhorn Press, 2007.

Ereira, Alan. *The Elder Brother Speaks: A Lost South American People and Their Message about the Fate of the Earth.* New York: Knopf, 1992.

Halifax, Joan. *The Fruitful Darkness: Reconnecting with the Body of the Earth.* San Francisco: HarperSanFrancisco, 1993.

Hanh, Thich Nhat. *The Miracle of Mindfulness.* Boston: Beacon Press, 1975.

Mindell, Arnold. *Dreambody: The Body's Role in Revealing the Self.* Boston: Sigo Press, 1982.

———. *The Shaman's Body: A New Shamanism for Transforming Health, Relationship, and the Community.* San Francisco: HarperSanFrancisco, 1993.

Noriega Rivera, Paco. *La Flora Medicinal de los Parques del Distrito Metrapolitan de Quito*. Quito, Ecuador: Abya-Yala, 2018.

Noriega Rivera, Patricia. *El Vuelo del Aguila y el Condor: Historia de Vida del Tayta Yachak Alberto Taxo*. Quito, Ecuador: Casa de la Cutura Ecuatoriana, 2015.

Perkins, John. *The World Is As You Dream It: Teachings from the Amazon and Andes*. Rochester, Vt.: Destiny Books, 1994.

Reichel-Domatoff, Gerardo. *The Sacred Mountain of Columbia's Kogi Indians*. Leiden, Netherlands: E.J. Brill, 1990.

Silko, Leslie Marmon. *Ceremony*. New York: Viking, 1977.

Tatzo, Alberto, and German Rodriguez. *Vision Cosmica de los Andes*. Quito: Abya-Yala Press, 1998.

Taxo, Don Alverto. *Invitation from the Andes: Entering the Wisdom of the Condor*. Ann Arbor, Mich.: Little Light, 2002.

———. *Friendship with the Elements: Opening the Channels of Communication*. Edited by Helen Slomovits. Ann Arbor, Mich.: Little Light, 2005.

Toelken, Barre. "Seeing with a Native Eye: How Many Sheep Does it Hold?" In *Seeing with a Native Eye: Essays on Native Religion*. Edited by Walter Holden Capps. New York: Harper and Row, 1976.

Wordsworth, William. "Ode: Intimations of Immortality from Recollections of Early Childhood." In *The Collected Poems of William Wordsworth*. London: Wordsworth Editions, 1998.

INDEX